SOPHOCLES THE DRAMATIST

SOPHOCLES
THE DRAMATIST

BY

A. J. A. WALDOCK

*Late Challis Professor of English Literature
in the University of Sydney*

CAMBRIDGE
AT THE UNIVERSITY PRESS
1966

PUBLISHED BY

THE SYNDICS OF THE CAMBRIDGE UNIVERSITY PRESS

Bentley House, 200 Euston Road, London, N.W.1
American Branch: 32 East 57th Street, New York, N.Y. 10022
West African Office: P.M.B. 5181, Ibadan, Nigeria

First published 1951
reprinted 1966
First paperback edition 1966

First printed in Great Britain by The Carlyle Press, Birmingham, 6
Reprinted in Great Britain by lithography by
Butler & Tanner Ltd, Frome and London

CONTENTS

PREFACE

THE assumption upon which this book is written is that Sophocles was first and foremost a dramatist. This assumption seems to me to be confirmed by nearly every line that he wrote. It is shaken only by an occasional stanza in which it is evident that Sophocles the dramatist has for the moment, and without any reservations, yielded to Sophocles the lyric poet—in which Sophocles seems to become oblivious of his drama and writes verses that actually conflict with it. But these moments of complete dramatic forgetfulness are not, after all, very frequent. In the main, Sophocles writes dramas; that is his paramount preoccupation; all his intentness is on that. It follows that what he has to say as a wise man will be incidental to what he is about as a dramatist. It follows, too, that in his fortunes as a dramatist we may expect to find ups and downs. Dramatists are not always at their peak, they do not move on a perpetual high plateau of accomplishment. They fluctuate in their 'form', are lucky or less lucky with their themes. If we could explore at will amongst the lost plays perhaps we should not again fail to think of Sophocles as human. In any case, it does no good to the work of any artist to approach it with bated breath. Sophocles becomes at once, I think, much more interesting if we take him as a writer among writers, expecting to find differences of quality and admitting the differences we see.

This raises the question of the seeing. It is my conviction that, faced with a drama, a group of cultivated people see the same thing—that there is little significant variation between one natural response and another. I develop in the following pages this doctrine of the 'natural response'. Variations from it usually arise because something has intervened to provoke an artificial response; and I think that the chances of such intervention rise steeply with increase in scholarship. The matter is obviously important; I make some inquiry into it in the Part that immediately follows.

SYDNEY, APRIL 1949   A.J.A.W.

PUBLISHERS' NOTE

PROFESSOR WALDOCK finished the manuscript of this book only a few months before his death, after a brief illness, in January 1950. The publishers express their gratitude to Mr R. G. Howarth, Reader in English Literature in the University of Sydney, who has corrected the proofs and seen the book through the press.

PART I

CRITICAL CANONS

CHAPTER I

THE HISTORICAL METHOD
AND ITS LIMITATIONS

IF modern scholarship is sure of one thing it is that criticism must be 'historical'. We can never really know a writer, it says, until we know his time; only when we have done our utmost to think as his age thought, to feel as his age felt, are we entitled to think that we know what *he* thought and felt; only then can we venture an estimate of the true significance of his work.

This is a great change, and a good one, since the days when anybody felt perfectly free to extract whatever meaning seemed to him appropriate from Shakespeare, Sophocles, Homer or anybody else. Yet there is another side to it, and perhaps the time has come when the basic validities of the historical approach need to be reviewed.

It is possible, I think, to make certain distinctions. There are cases where special information is indispensable, where we could blunder badly if we lacked it, where the whole drift of a passage or scene could escape us if we came to it unequipped with a particular set of facts about the past. My feeling is that such passages are rarer than is often thought, but they exist. An example occurs in the prayer scene in *Hamlet*: the soliloquy that Hamlet utters when he comes on Claudius at his devotions:

Now might I do it pat, now he is praying;
And now I'll do't; and so he goes to heaven;
And so am I revenged: that would be scann'd:
A villain kills my father; and for that,
I, his sole son, do this same villain send
To heaven.
O, this is hire and salary, not revenge.
He took my father grossly, full of bread;
With all his crimes broad blown, as flush as May;
And how his audit stands who knows save heaven?
But, in our circumstance and course of thought,
'Tis heavy with him: and am I then revenged,
To take him in the purging of his soul,
When he is fit and season'd for his passage?
No.
Up, sword; and know thou a more horrid hent:
When he is drunk asleep, or in his rage . . .
At gaming, swearing, or about some act
That has no relish of salvation in't;
Then trip him, that his heels may kick at heaven,
And that his soul may be as damn'd and black
As hell, whereto it goes. My mother stays:
This physic but prolongs thy sickly days.[1]

Certain questions arise from this passage, and a good deal hinges on the answers to them. Does Hamlet really *believe* what he says about sending his uncle's soul to hell? Does he think that it can be done, and is he in earnest about doing it? Or are his opening words, as A. C. Bradley thought, an indication that he has no 'effective desire' to kill the king, and is this impression confirmed by the 'repulsive', incredible talk about hell? The fact seems to be that we cannot answer these questions by our unaided, twentieth-century intelligence, nor is our sympathetic imagination, in this

[1] Act III, Sc. 3, ll. 73-98.

particular instance, enough. We need information. We need to know what were the current Elizabethan beliefs about heaven and hell and prayer. On the basis of this knowledge we need to reconstruct the probable response of the Elizabethan audience to the passage, and on the basis of this, again, to form an estimate of what Shakespeare himself probably intended the passage to convey. The results may be disappointing, even uninteresting, compared with the subtle conclusions that our unhampered intelligences can draw; but, for all that, it is very likely that they will be true.

I doubt, however, if there are many passages, whether in Elizabethan drama or in Greek, that confront us with so critical a choice as this—if there are many passages in which, for default of historical information, we could so completely miss the cue. As a rule, we catch the drift, come within reasonable distance of the mark; it is a question, after that, of refining our responses, of attaining, as far as in us lies, ever closer approximations to the truth.

In the study of Greek drama, what special information do we require in order that we may try, with the best advantage, to make our reception of its meaning exact? The information, I suppose, is somewhat of this kind: we need to be informed about the place of women in the home and in society; about the relationships of fathers and sons and of brothers and sisters; about the bonds of family in general; about the friendships of young men, and about romantic love as this was known to the Greeks. We need information, also, about certain rites that have vanished from our scene, or that have somewhat changed their meaning: one of these is the rite of supplication, another is the rite of burial. We have to learn, as well, to accord full weight to feelings that have become a little strange: the feeling, for example, that it can be as much a matter of duty to hate as to love, to be harsh to one's enemies as to be kind to one's friends. It is important, also, to know how the Greeks felt about luck—and about walking softly to avert ill-luck: to understand how deep in their being was the sense of the ill-omened word, and how serious a consideration to them was all that we so lightly imply in our maxim 'touch wood'. We arrive at a knowledge of these matters with varying ease; what is essential could reach us unconsciously, no doubt, in a reading of six Greek plays. However it reaches us, such knowledge all bears on one main end: to help us to see the work as it was and is. To assist us in these efforts is the function of the historical critic.

So far so good. But the historical critic is not always content to stop at this point. He is rather like a zealot who cannot cease in performing good works, or a conjurer who, having begun to draw the ribbon from the hat, keeps on drawing it out, yard by yard, for pure delight in his craft. The historical critic, in a similar way, often seems bemused by the zest of his calling. Illustration is in his blood, and he will continue to furnish his 'proofs' long after the point has been reached when anything remains to be proved. Consider, for example, this list of theses about the thoughts and feelings of the Greeks; Greek drama would certainly suggest that they are true, but historical criticism has been reluctant to take any single one of them for granted. Each has been carefully inquired into, rigorously tested, checked and then checked again by the evidence. The average Greek thought and felt these things: that parents should be respected; that marriage is desirable; that girls who miss marriage are unfortunate; that friends ought to be loyal to one another;

4

that in military matters discipline is good; that generals, accordingly, should be treated with some deference, and, other things being equal, should be obeyed; that the best men never seem to come back from a war; that great success can bring insecurity; that from dizzy heights one can have bad falls; that life is a series of ups and downs. As I say, each of these theses has been closely probed, and only after full documentation has been passed as true: now that the evidence is all in and the parallels gathered, we may safely assume that the Greeks really did think and feel these things. May not one fairly suggest that in corroboration carried to such lengths a faint tinge of superfluity lurks? Is there not some forgetfulness here of what we may reasonably consider to be the chief of all historical facts: that man has remained much the same?

Historical criticism is guilty at times, however, of something a little worse than excess. It can, on occasion, actually hinder, it can clog and hamper instead of help. There are times when one feels that its instruments are blunt—that the understanding, by itself, has a finer edge—or when one feels that it is a net of too coarse a mesh through which all that really matters is slipping away. I mention, merely for the moment, three cases. Oedipus, after the terrible disclosure that is the climax of the *Tyrannus*, retires from the stage; while he is absent he puts out his eyes. What is to be our verdict on this act of self-mutilation? The view that we should blame Oedipus dates back a long way, and it is possible, by use of maxims, to lend it much plausible colour. But here, surely, is a case where maxims can only be a nuisance—or worse—for they could easily end by ruining the play. Here only one authority exists—the drama; let us submit to the drive of the drama and the question becomes at once unreal. Consider, again, Antigone's act—unconventional, rash, without precedent. Was it, in truth, unwomanly of her to assert herself so vigorously in a masculine world? Aristotle thought—or pretended to think—that women should be meek, submissive and quiet. Many men after him have thought, or pretended to think, the same. So, without much trouble (seeing that from men themselves have come nine-tenths of all pronouncements on women) it is possible to build up for this period (as for any) a formidable-seeming body of opinion. This puts us into something of a dilemma, for it is hard for us to censure Antigone: hard to feel, at any point of the drama, that her sister Ismēne sets off womanhood to better advantage. The case is perhaps less critical than at first it might seem, but the historical method, with its disquieting citations, can make us for a moment very nervous. The matter is complex and must be reserved for fuller discussion; but this much may be said, that here again we must be prepared to stand our ground and resist the seeming force of illustration. So, once more, with Deianira. Deianira, to win back her husband, resorted, disastrously, to magic. It is possible, without any doubt, to construct a heavy indictment against her, yet perhaps authority here also may be questioned.

I would suggest, then, that the historical method runs various risks; and I think too (a point at which I have hinted) that it is a method particularly apt to defeat its own ends. It stands in a slight but a constant danger of asserting history only, in the upshot, to deny it. There is the problem, for example, of the audience. This problem, indeed, is crucial; if we go seriously astray here there is no limit to the mistakes we may make. Now I would suggest, due allowances made, that there is only one assumption in this matter that has the slightest claim to historical point; it is the assumption that a typical Greek audience was very like a modern in sympathy, responsiveness, and the nature of the enjoyment it expected to find. There are hints that this really was so. It is one of the charms of the *Poetics* to feel within that sober treatise a faint but very perceptible effusion of the Athenian theatre in action. In his casual names, his casual references, Aristotle brings it tantalizingly close: we seem to be almost within earshot of it all. And do we not feel instinctive kinship with the audiences whose excitements and murmurings we seem almost to catch in his pages? We feel that we know why Agathon was popular: he would be popular, we feel, with us. We may think that the critics of Euripides were unfair, but we can almost hear them muttering (in the very style of their counterparts of today): 'Why go to the theatre to be harrowed? There is worry enough in life as it is.' These Greek audiences surmised through Aristotle seem, after all, very like our own. Yet how different is the impression they make when Professor Bowra[1] re-creates them! Professor Bowra's gift of illustration is notable—no scholar surpasses him in it—yet the audience whose wraith one half-sees in his pages is unlike any that one has ever known. This audience does not seem on enjoyment bent: its mood is much more serious and sombre. One suspects it of having brought along with it its sets of Aristotle, Thucydides and Pindar; if not, it has arrived word-perfect in the works of those writers, and waits ready to make instant application of its knowledge. The dramatists must have hated this audience, for it is

[1] Now Sir Maurice Bowra.

essentially an audience that nags. It is a terribly vigilant audience: an audience much given to 'mistrusting', and to having doubts about the conduct of characters. It is an audience quite weighed down by its duties, an audience with a watching brief for the best standards of Athenian life. It is indeed in all respects so awkward an audience that the query is constantly occurring to one why the dramatists wrote so many plays for it. It is, in effect, so 'unhistorical' an audience that we may feel quite sure that it never existed.

It is not cavilling to make one further point, not against historical criticism as such, but in allusion to certain drawbacks that seem inherent in its nature. The effect of it, nearly always, is to reduce the stature of its subject. For instance, some years ago Miss Lily Campbell wrote a book on the tragic heroes of Shakespeare. It incorporates much important material, and Miss Campbell's point of view has its interest. Yet many chapters of this book (to me at least) are depressing, because they seem to offer the shells of Shakespeare's dramas with everything that we most valued left out. Miss Campbell's object is to spin connections between Shakespeare and the moral philosophy of his day; her thesis is that each tragedy is essentially a study of passion—*Hamlet* is a study in grief, *King Lear* is a study in wrath, and so on. There is much that is illuminating here, and yet the net result of it all seems to be to leave us with a sort of formula where previously we had a play. The tragedies become large diagrams; stock emotions, not people, seem to make them. And Miss Campbell shows us again what is likely to happen when illustration takes charge. Surely all ordinary persons will concede that *King Lear* is a straightforward play; it is great, but the feelings in it are simple. Must we be versed in strange experiences before we can understand what this play is about? The elements of it are all around us, every suburb can show its issues in miniature. Why then must we summon philosophers to help us, why resort to the wise men of old? For example, do we really need Seneca's guidance? Seneca said that ' a first cause of unthankfulness' is to pick out the wrong people for our benefits. No one would quarrel with the dictum; but can a sociological observation of this quality conceivably shed light on the experiences of Lear? Seneca also committed himself to the view that 'a man is angered by an injury to his self-esteem'. The thought may have occurred to ourselves. Have we so little confidence in our judgments that we must refer, in all solemnity, to Seneca before we venture to apply this opinion to *Lear*?

But the constant appeal to authority can be something worse than a rather ineffectual game; it can cramp the processes of criticism, it can restrict and twist and distort. 'Slave of habitual wrath'—that was one of the conceptions of moral philosophers, and if we are applying moral philosophy to *Lear* it is natural to make for the phrase. But what good can possibly come from the tag? What service have we rendered to criticism when we have labelled Lear with that formula? It is not even as if the formula fitted him—it does not, of course, come within reach of the truth of him. It is the same when, on identical lines, we attempt to explain the motives of his actions. Plutarch once grappled with the problem: why is it that old men retire? They themselves usually say 'old age', but that is merely their cunning, said Plutarch. Old men generally retire through laziness, and are much to be censured for doing so: they should stay for a much longer time at their posts and take their due part in the work of the world. Miss Campbell seizes on this: another key to another problem in *Lear*! Why did Lear take it into his head to abdicate? Plutarch *dixit*: 'Voluptuousness and sloth.' Miss Campbell has plenty of penetration of her own; it is entirely unnecessary for her to lean on these sages; but between Plutarch and Seneca she seems helpless; in the grip of the historical obsession she follows humbly wherever they lead.

There is no question of rejecting the historical method, but there is a real reason for keeping it in its place, and especially for resisting the preposterous assumption that any work more than a few hundred years old must baffle us unless we have authorities constantly at our elbow.

CHAPTER II

THE DOCUMENTARY FALLACY

I USE this phrase—the best I can think of—to indicate one of the commonest, and perhaps also one of the most serious, of all critical errors. It is an error, curiously enough, that besets simple and sophisticated alike; and yet its incidence, when all is said, is perhaps not so curious, for it may almost be regarded as a natural (though mistaken) by-product of literary appeal.

I will give a recent instance—perhaps a somewhat extravagant one—of the kind of aberration I have in mind. In the *Yale Review* for Spring 1946, there appeared an article by Mr Harold Goddard with the title 'In Ophelia's Closet'. Mr Goddard explained that he was, in effect, elaborating an idea presented to him some years previously by a student. 'A young mind, unprejudiced by the critics and commentators, has a freshness that makes its spontaneous impressions worthy of notice.' The student had 'offered an interpretation of a passage in *Hamlet* so startlingly original, yet so simple and in many ways convincing, that I was astounded that no one, so far as I knew, had ever thought of it before'. The passage in question was this:

Polonius. How now, Ophelia! what's the matter?
Ophelia. O, my lord, my lord, I have been so affrighted!
Polonius. With what, i' the name of God?
Ophelia. My lord, as I was sewing in my closet,

Lord Hamlet, with his doublet all unbraced,
No hat upon his head, his stockings foul'd,
Ungarter'd and down-gyved to his ancle;
Pale as his shirt, his knees knocking each other;
And with a look so piteous in purport
As if he had been loosed out of hell
To speak of horrors—he comes before me.
Polonius. Mad for thy love?
Ophelia. My lord, I do not know;
But, truly, I do fear it.
Polonius.   What said he?
Ophelia. He took me by the wrist and held me hard;
Then goes he to the length of all his arm;
And, with his other hand thus o'er his brow,
He falls to such perusal of my face
As he would draw it. Long stay'd he so;
At last, a little shaking of mine arm
And thrice his head thus waving up and down,
He raised a sigh so piteous and profound,
As it did seem to shatter all his bulk
And end his being: that done, he lets me go:
And, with his head over his shoulder turn'd,
He seem'd to find his way without his eyes;
For out o' doors he went without their helps,
And, to the last, bended their light on me.
Polonius. Come, go with me: I will go seek the king.
This is the very ecstasy of love,
Whose violent property fordoes itself,
And leads the will to desperate undertakings,
As oft as any passion under heaven
That does afflict our natures. I am sorry.
What, have you given him any hard words of late?
Ophelia. No, my good lord; but, as you did command,
I did repel his letters, and denied
His access to me.
Polonius.   That hath made him mad.[1]

[1] Act II, Sc. 1, ll. 74-110.

Mr Goddard rightly remarks that this extraordinary interview 'has been the occasion of much critical puzzlement and disagreement', and proceeds then to the point of his article. 'Well, the student to whom I have referred proposed to cut the Gordian knot of all these difficulties at one stroke. He suggested that Hamlet never made any such visit to Ophelia's closet and that the whole thing was a daydream or hallucination—the first clear symptom of the insanity that finally overwhelmed her.'

Mr Goddard goes on to adduce certain reasons that seem to him to lend support to this theory. Ophelia is in love for the first time and encounters parental obstruction. Her emotions, in consequence, are dammed up, and because these repressed emotions are associated with a sense of guilt she is in a highly fit state to have dreams, daydreams, reveries— and (why not?) hallucinations. Again, she was alone, sewing, at the time when she says Hamlet appeared to her. Solitude and monotony! 'What conditions could be more favourable for such a visitation?' Once again, is not Ophelia's account of the interview 'eerie'? 'He comes before me', she says; not 'entered' the room, not 'broke into it'. It is an odd phrase to use of a person, but it is 'exactly what an apparition does'. Hamlet's withdrawal, also, is 'eerie'; and how is this to be explained? Dover Wilson sees in his pantomime—in that silent coming and going—suggestions of the kind of mood that can supervene on some terrible dream or nightmare. Mr Goddard says 'Exactly, but whose?' and proceeds:

Wilson attributes the nightmarish atmosphere wholly to Hamlet's conduct, not at all to Ophelia's fright. Surely that is wrong under any interpretation. A coldly objective account of insane behaviour is one thing, a highly emotional one is another. It is the latter that we have here, as Ophelia's 'so affrighted' is enough to prove. Moreover, strong suspicion is thrown on the trustworthiness of her story by the fact that nowhere else in the play does Hamlet behave even remotely as he is represented as behaving in this scene. Who can doubt that the frightened and guilt-obsessed Ophelia exaggerated? The only question is, how much? The fear that begins by overstating may end by creating outright.[1]

It is hardly necessary to continue, and it would be absurd to embark on any serious refutation of the arguments brought forward in this article. Some of them are based purely and simply on misstatements of fact, like the one in the passage just quoted. Ophelia is upset, naturally; her heart is still beating fast; but she is not hysterical, she is not beside herself, she is not in a panic, and she is not mentally confused. Far from it. Her account is as objective as one could well expect; it is not quite '*coldly* objective', but in the circumstances it is remarkably cool. It is a thoroughly lucid, detailed, clear-headed narrative, and of course to anyone responding naturally it carries an immediate conviction of truth. But, as I say, it would be superfluous to argue the matter. The preposterousness of Mr Goddard's theory is all-pervasive, complete and ingrained.

The principle exemplified here is surely very simple. Good literature, we all know, is 'real'; literature reaches us through illusion, and on the strength of this illusion a great many of its merits depend. But a piece of imaginative writing is one thing, a sequence of actual events quite another. There is nothing in Mr Goddard's thesis that is inherently absurd, nothing cranky or improbable in his

[1] *Op. cit.*, pp. 466-7.

reasonings as such; the absurdity lies in the unconscious premise from which all these reasonings proceed. The premise is that *Hamlet* is a document: that it is a literal transcript of fact: that it somehow records what, at that given time and place, an interlinked set of people said and did. This is the concealed assumption; and once this assumption is made it is clear that Mr Goddard's line of inquiry is perfectly right. Indeed, his investigation could have been much more searching and thorough: all the instruments of historical research, all the power of modern psychology, might justifiably be brought to bear, not merely on this one scene, but on every issue raised by the play. For it is obvious that—such an assumption once made—the whole ground of the inquiry is shifted. A document, preserving by some miraculous means the record of what really took place, would open up endless possibilities of conjecture; not a trifle, not the obscurest detail, but might be the key to the ultimate truth.

What renders Mr Goddard's thesis, and every thesis of this nature, ridiculous is the simple fact that a play is a work of art: a piece of writing most carefully put together in order that it may achieve a most carefully calculated effect. A play —or a novel, or any other creative work presenting an action—is by no means a flat documentary text; it is a complex of most subtle highlights and lowlights. It is compounded of shading and relief, its very being consists in intricate emphases and suppressions; and in a sense—unlike life—it has no depth. Literature operates on a thinnish crust, and there is nothing underneath this crust. Any piece of fact has depth beyond depth underlying it. Our instruments of research may be weak, our discoveries, after all our efforts, meagre, but the depths are assuredly there. In literature, by contrast, *appearance* is everything, and there is no reality below the appearance. The documentary critic is always seeking to 'get to the bottom' of a piece of literature, in much the same way as he would seek to get to the bottom of a piece of life; but, with literature, there is no bottom to be reached. The crust is all; beneath this crust there is nothing.

Consider for a moment *King Lear*. We know a good deal about Lear the man; we feel his personality very intensely; in a sense he is more real to us than most of the people we know. But we do not know what he fancied for his dinner, we do not know what a modern electrocardiograph would have revealed of the condition of his heart, we do not know (though this perhaps we could guess) what sort of a chairman he made at his council meetings; and it is not the slightest use our trying to find out these things. Again, and a little more seriously: somewhere in the background was a wife—or would have been if this tale had been true—and this wife, in the realm of fact, would have been a figure of real importance. Her influence might have accounted for much, and in ways beyond her control she could hardly have helped having her share in the intricate network of causation that would have produced the events of *King Lear*. Even if she had died long years before these events took place, still it would have been helpful to know of her nature. Historically considered, it would have been *necessary* to know of her nature, for without such knowledge no estimate could possibly have been complete. But in our drama Lear's wife is not even in the background; for the purpose of the drama it is as if she never existed; yet the scheme of the play is complete.

Or there is the question of minor characters. In life also there is a contrast of major and minor; but in life men are major and minor in the significance of the parts they play, not in the degree of existence they have—the measure in which they are really in being. In a play, on the other hand, a set of characters can be a hierarchy, and it is not a question merely of the relative importance of their parts. They can differ in the extent to which they are *there*, in the actual measure of life they possess. Suppose we approach a play as if it were some historical text: immediately these degrees begin to diminish, the temptation is to give each character his full quota of substantial life; and it is astonishing how far this process will go. The reader will perhaps recall the name 'Camillo' as that of a character in *The Winter's Tale*. It would not be altogether surprising if he did not recall it, for this Camillo is barely existent. He is useful in the plot, but his personal impact is nil. He is possessed of a few type-qualities; we classify him without trouble; we know the general kind of man he is; but beyond this outline there is nothing. Yet Camillo has come in for his share of 'character-studies', and I know of one such account that is masterly. In this the writer has brought to life a character that would have pleased and astonished Shakespeare—might even have pro-voked his envy. This critic possessed a very rich creative gift and he has done nothing less than re-conceive Camillo. His approach is documentary throughout. He takes the whole play as so much evidence. Then by using Camillo's words for texts and making them starting-points for intricate deductions, he conjures up a character from the void. It is a fascinating reconstruction—one that, as I say, might have given deep pleasure to Shakespeare himself. And if *The*

Winter's Tale, instead of being a drama, had been a literal record of things said and done, the reconstruction might well have been true.

In summary, I make the point once again, that in reading literature our impressions are everything and that outside them there is nothing to be found. I do not suggest for a moment that we are not entitled to think our impressions over; their reception can in itself be a difficult matter, and it may be necessary for us to check and re-check them with infinite care. But we should be watchful of the manner in which we think them over (for it is here that the danger lurks): making it our utmost effort to abide by them; not attempting (except in restrained and cautious ways) to supplement them; above all, not seeking to go behind them, for there is nothing behind them but delusion.

The flowering time of the documentary fallacy was in the later years of the nineteenth century and the early years of the present. It was strongly evident in German commentary on Shakespeare, it coloured most of the Shakespearian writings of A. C. Bradley; but the high priest of the cult was Verrall. Verrall was the transcendent documentarian.

The reaction against Verrall has been strong enough, I suppose, to render any detailed comment on his technique unnecessary, but there are still classic object-lessons to be drawn from his pages. He has whole paragraphs of elucidations so fantastic that they could easily have been written in caricature of his method by some satirist setting out ingeniously to mock it. His study of the *Heracles,* for example, could serve almost from start to finish for such a parody. There is no space for any detailed illustration from this, and in any case it would be superfluous to give it. But consider the fashion in which Verrall sets about disposing of the deeds of the hero: it is in the spirit of the most sceptical historian. It is true, says Verrall, that we have Heracles' own word for these wonders, but how much is this word worth, how far are we entitled to trust it? Deianira, certainly, we may accept as an eye-witness: she saw Heracles wrestle down and defeat that monstrous god of the river. This testimony is to be believed as far as it goes, but what of all the other items in the legend? Verrall bids us note how the hero's own friends falter when put to the test, how sorry, for example, is the showing of Amphitryon when cross-examined by the hostile Lycus. Amphitryon has almost nothing to reply: cannot produce one genuine informant, cannot offer one single precise and duly certified instance. Instead, there is airy talk: of centaurs (unavailable, naturally, for questioning), battles with gods ('of which we are not told so much as the place'), awful contests with giants (for which not a shred of proof is forthcoming). And if Amphitryon's case breaks down, what better account of the matter can the Chorus give? It praises, but of what value as evidence is praise? No, the fact is, says Verrall, that on every hand it is hearsay we meet; everywhere there is this paucity of documentation; everything rests on the flimsiest report. The single exception is Heracles' war with the Amazons, but as to that, Verrall warns us to be doubly on guard. That war may indeed have occurred, but let us not fall dupe to a common trick of the lawyers, and, because this one allegation turns out to be true, be induced to relax in our suspicion of the others: 'The narrators prove what is credible, and then, with a logic not unfamiliar to us, demand credence for things which are not.'

Verrall's scrutinies force him steadily towards one conclusion. He asks us to note the demeanour of Heracles in the early scenes of the play. Is there not a strangeness in the hero's air? Is it a lucid Heracles we see? Could we regard him *now* as an altogether credible witness?

But what then of those other reminiscences and reports, with which in times past he may be presumed to have occasionally nourished the faith of favourable recipients, such as the doting father and the venerable as well as venerating friends? What was the state of mind, when he related, as sometimes he apparently did, that the water-snakes of Lerna were all one snake, one beast with ten thousand necks, that a Thracian chief kept horses whose mangers were supplied with human flesh, that there were horsemen in Arcadia, three-bodied men in Erytheia, and beyond that, if you went far, far towards and into the setting sun, there were —what was there not? What part of these travels had he really made, and what things had he truly found? The doubt, the suspicion, which cover this last voyage to Taenarum, are seen, when we reflect, to spread backwards over everything which he may have been led to say of himself, especially in the unguarded freedom of intimacy and the domestic circle.[1]

Or take, for a second brief instance, Verrall's treatment of Iris and Madness. These two beings appear suddenly above the palace: their coming heralds the breakdown of Heracles. Verrall, of course, refuses point-blank to accept them as 'real': that would have thrown his whole view of the Euripidean drama awry. Somehow or other they must be visions. But if visions, who is it that has them? Verrall, casting around, sees that only the Chorus can perform this function: it is the Chorus that dream Iris and Madness. And if one looks very closely into the text, says Verrall, one sees

[1] *Four Plays of Euripides* (1905), p. 160.

that there really are some indications of this. The Chorus make stupid remarks when the messenger comes in to tell of the horrors—almost as if they have completely forgotten what Iris prophesied only a few moments before. That, says Verrall, is exactly the case: a dreamer wakes from his dream and forgets it; the Chorus rouse themselves from their visions and, lo, the visions have faded, leaving no remembrance behind. But a possible objector might ask: just what was the mechanism of these visions, and how, in particular, did it come about that a *group* of men were able to dream them? Did the Chorus dream their dream jointly, with perfect synchronization? Verrall is pressed, but still far from defeated. It was not precisely a group-dream; there was a kind of dreamer-in-chief; and in any case, he adds (blessed refuge-word for the critic in trouble!) it was symbol. But, again, when exactly was it they dreamed? A dream implies sleep; are we to understand that at some given signal this Chorus (again with perfect synchronization) dropped into slumber? Is there any sign in the text that they did? There is a patch of dialogue, answers Verrall, that looks very like it: a patch in which their thought becomes very 'abrupt'; and this was 'accompanied doubtless by corresponding changes in the music and action'. So the weary ones gradually drop off, sinking down here and there in the sleep of old age. 'Then and not till then, their chief, who plays the dreamer, betrays his inward agitation by a start and a cry "See, O see!"... and overhead the forms of his daydream roll forth into air.'[1]

One can only marvel at such writing. From the whole of critical literature would it be easy to match such a passage?

[1] *Op. cit.*, p. 172.

Yet it is not remarkably out of the way for Verrall; many other rationalizations are almost equally extreme. Even so, Verrall had his brilliance as a critic, and to this day it is not safe to ignore him. He has many observations that are shrewd, and some that we may still feel to be profound. But his original angle of vision was wrong. Because his pursuit of his method was unflinching, he is the outstanding example in criticism of the monstrous distortions that can follow from one initial slight error in approach. He was rapt away by the dramas he studied; that was good, but he studied them in a sort of oblivion. He had lost, in the proliferation of his ideas, all sense of what a drama is; had forgotten, in the fascination of his research, the very ABC of the ways in which every drama must work. I always feel that there was a cure waiting for Verrall, if only it had occurred to him to take it. If he had seen a few more dramas in action I am convinced that the whole drift of his criticism would have changed. A short course of intensive theatre-going, and Verrall would have glimpsed the comedy underlying his whole attitude to drama; six visits even to the music-halls of his day, and Verrall would have burst into laughter at his theories.

Since Verrall, the documentary fallacy has been pruned of its wilder extravagances. Now and again, it is true, it burgeons forth in something of its pristine glory; an article like Mr Goddard's can remind us of the efflorescences of former days. On the whole, however, it has become more sedate, operates now with a more deceptive discretion. But it would be a great error to think that it is not still with us. There are various signs by which one may come to know it—types of phrase that herald its presence. 'May we not fairly conjure up a background?' 'Do we not behind all this catch a glimpse?' Expressions of this kind should warn us that the documentary fallacy is near. The second quotation is from Professor G. M. A. Grube, and I may leave the subject for the present with the briefest reference to the case it concerns. Mr Grube is discussing the *Hippolytus* and is emphasizing the illegitimate birth of the hero. He inclines to see in this fact the secret roots of the young man's character, so that, as Mr Grube interprets it, bastardy is at the very heart of the tragedy. As a bastard Hippolytus 'was not Theseus' heir and his position in the family is unhappy, or at least would have been in the fifth century'.[1] (There is a danger signal in the last part of this sentence.) Mr Grube then surveys the text, on the look-out for signs that Hippolytus, as a bastard, really was neglected, put upon, disparaged. He discovers two or three: the nurse calls him the 'bastard son'; Phaedra twice calls him 'the son of the Amazon'; and there are one or two other references as colourless. Presently Mr Grube is picturing for us 'the boy, abandoned by his father, ashamed of his mother, thrown more and more upon himself until he is forced to cultivate that aloofness of which he is so proud'. It is to be stressed that such a picture is contrary to every impression of Euripides' tragedy. Is there the slightest clear suggestion in the drama that Hippolytus, because of his bastardy, has suffered? Every indication points precisely in the opposite way. The nurse seems to think that it is the illegitimate son who may cloud the future of the legitimate heirs. What Mr Grube is really doing is trying to improve Euripides' drama: to make it cohere, perhaps, a little more tightly, to impart to it some additional depth. His idea, in itself, is attractive: but how if this idea

[1] *The Drama of Euripides* (1941), p. 184.

does not appear in the play? The play seems to make no special point of the irregular birth of Hippolytus. It recognizes it, but without underlining it. It most certainly does not bring it into relief, it gives it no weight in the scheme of events. If that is the natural impression, then a fanciful filling-in can only do harm, and arguments from fifth-century bastardy will only confuse the clear effect of the play.

CHAPTER III

PATTERN-MAKING

'ENGLAND distrusts generalizations': so Professor Nikolaus Pevsner begins a recent article on the special style of architecture called 'Mannerism'.[1] 'The tendency is to treat each case on its own merits and leave the perfection of codes of law to more logical and less practical nations.'

The words raise an interesting issue. We need not trouble about their accuracy as a summation of national character, but they certainly underline a contrast in critical attitudes. There are critics (and they are by no means exclusively English) who have an instinctive preference for taking cases as they come, and who find uneasiness creeping on them in the presence of generalizations of more than moderate reach. There are other critics (of whom Mr Pevsner is one) whose breath of life is the generalization, and who have a feeling that they are wasting their own and their readers' time unless they can bring a huge diversity of detail into a system of quite staggering breadth.

Mr Pevsner offers his article on Mannerism as a small example or model of the kind of criticism that reaches what he describes as 'broad conclusions'. Mr Pevsner's perceptiveness, without any question, is extraordinary, and his elucidation—so far as it concerns detail—entrancing. But the detail merely leads up to the main matter. Mr Pevsner

[1] In *The Mint*, ed. Geoffrey Grigson (1946).

asks himself the question: what is the inner meaning of Mannerism? 'How can this self-conscious dissenting, frustrated style be accounted for? What made such opposed characters as Michelangelo and Giulio Romano evolve it and the Popes and the Jesuits welcome it?'[1] He proceeds then to answer the question. In a series of generalizations that must give any reader of the distrustful kind a passing sensation of vertigo, in a series of deductive leaps that would have made even Ruskin blench, he 'demonstrates' that Michelangelo, Giulio Romano, Pius V, Ignatius Loyola, St Charles Borromeo, the Inquisition, the wars of religion, Nonconformity and the censorship of books were all expressions of the same spiritual mood. The world of 1530 to 1600 was a 'split world'—'a period of tormenting doubt, and rigorous enforcement of no longer self-understood dogma'.[2] Mr Pevsner discerns linkages in every direction: the frigidity of Michelangelo; the pornography of Aretino; the lack of predominant accent in the Collegio Romano; the inconsistencies in the façade of the Palazzo Bevilacqua; Vignola's failure to make the bottom storeys of buildings agree with the top: such assorted phenomena as these, along with the Inquisition, the Jesuits and the exceptional proliferation of saints in this period, are seen by him merely as aspects of the one basic spiritual fact. It is true that before he finishes Mr Pevsner's confidence seems just perceptibly to falter; he admits that, after all, he may have been guilty of some slight degree of over-simplification. There is, for one instance, the question of the Elizabethan temperament and the problem of Elizabethan domestic architecture. How, precisely, do these fit into the pattern? How are we to

[1] *The Mint*, p. 132.   [2] *Ibid.* p. 136.

explain in terms of *Manierismus* 'the buoyance and sturdy strength of Elizabethan building'—qualities so different from those that Mr Pevsner has just been revealing in the Italian architecture of the time? Mr Pevsner is not unduly disturbed; after all, 'one should not expect criteria of style always to be applicable to different countries without national modifications';[1] Elizabethan architecture might yet turn out to be no exception. That seems to be the note on which Mr Pevsner concludes. Give him a little time (he seems to be saying) and he will undertake to reduce even Elizabethan architecture to *Manierismus*—to show that it too, despite its seeming recalcitrance, may be coaxed, with not too much thrusting, into the fold.

Mr Pevsner's gifts need no emphasizing here: his analyses are a constant delight. But may one not fairly detect beneath the whole drift of such an article something like an obsession with the idea of uniformity? Mr Pevsner's writing betrays a passion—almost a pathological craze—for reducing many things to one thing, for discovering resemblance in difference: one is tempted to say, for annihilating differences in order that he may establish, at all costs, a sameness.

It is a tendency, of course, easily understood. A piece of writing like this article may show the tendency in abnormal development, but one can sympathize with the desire that gives rise to it. It is a relief to bring multifarious facts into harmony; it gives the sensation of achieving truth. Yet it may be an illusory sensation. In the criticism of literature, at any rate, there are many sham systems in vogue. They seem systems, but look into them a little more closely, and they will often appear as rigidities forced on diversities. Perhaps

---

[1] *The Mint*, p. 137.

in criticism there are few temptations stronger than the temptation to include within some wide-stretching theory a multitude of facts that at first perplex and confuse. If they can be so included, well and good: but it is worth while to look very closely to see that the divergences are not being smothered, that the variety does truly yield to a pattern, that the multiplicity of the detail is not just being crowded into a scheme.

The matter is genuinely important, and deserves, I think, some slight illustration and discussion. It will be easiest if I offer at once some examples of what I take to be 'pattern-making'.

There is the Bradleian conception of tragedy. A. C. Bradley's theories of tragedy derive, of course, very largely from Hegel's: they are a modification or an adaptation of Hegel's. Hegel's views on tragedy fell (as one might have known they would) into the shape of a most beautiful system, but even Bradley felt that the more tragedies one actually read, the more one came to doubt the perfect satisfactoriness of the Hegelian scheme. So Bradley (without bating one jot of his admiration for Hegel) set himself to make certain slight adjustments, extensions and re-orderings in the master's design. In its central principle, however —that the essence of all tragedy is conflict—he made no change of any consequence. Bradley put the principle as follows. The conflict is between spiritual values. There are 'powers' in life to which it is natural for the human spirit to pay homage. The family and the state are such powers. So are certain relationships like the bond between brother and sister, the bond between husband and wife, the bond between citizen and ruler. Another kind of power is love;

so is the call of honour, or a man's devotion to a cause. Civilization is largely buttressed by such powers, and tragedy occurs when they clash. One power confronts another—the human spirit owing allegiance to both; it is then that the stage is set for the spectacle of the tragic collision. Each of the contending powers is a 'right', yet it is impossible for both to be fully asserted: 'the right of each is pushed into a wrong, because it ignores the right of the other'. The upshot of the tragic collision is waste and a 'denial of both the exclusive claims'.[1]

Here, then, is an impressive theory of tragedy. Bradley is not interested, it will be observed, in a conflict of right versus wrong. The less difference between the powers in rightness, the more piercingly tragic is the quarrel and the more terrible the ultimate issue. In reaffirming the Hegelian doctrines Bradley tried to keep in mind a somewhat larger assemblage of facts, and he obviously feels confidence in the scheme; he feels that no tragedy is likely to be put forward for which the theory will not adequately account.

Let us test it, then, on two examples, both of them often under Bradley's eye. *Romeo and Juliet* certainly supports it in part. It was one of the points of Hegel's theory that a truly tragic hero is completely absorbed. He gives his whole being to the power that moves him and this very plainly is Romeo's case; it is in this way that Romeo exists for his love. Here then is one power well shown. What constitutes the opposing force? Bradley takes it, of course, to be 'family': love and family are the competing powers, each (in his formula) pushing its right too far, so that each right is

[1] *Oxford Lectures on Poetry* (1911), p. 71.

transformed into wrong. At first glance this seems a very plausible scheme; but let us look a little more closely at the facts. What, in this context, does family amount to? We have not much direct knowledge of Montagues, but we are perfectly able to form an estimate of Capulets. Do these Capulets typify a very sacred 'value'? The shallow, neglectful mother, for whom her daughter scarcely exists; the kindly, but light-minded, father, without an inkling of the urgencies of the crisis: what sort of symbols for family are these? When Bradley and Hegel talk of 'forces' claiming allegiance we know perfectly well what they mean; but the forces must really be there—they must be genuine, they must really exist. In *Romeo and Juliet* one of them exists, but the other is no more than a name. The lovers are not fighting family, in the sense of a sanctified power, a power equal and opposite to their love. They are fighting selfishness and stupidity, an array of quite unsanctified values, to the reinforcement of which comes much sheer ill-luck. This is the truth of what happens in the play. Bradley, in short, has been deceived by a word—and by his overmastering desire for a pattern. The word 'family' seems to make a pair with 'love'—seems to represent a parallel value. In reality it does nothing of the kind, and the play of *Romeo and Juliet* quite escapes the Bradleian-Hegelian system.

Or consider the drama that was Hegel's own ever-recurring point of departure. In the *Antigone* there seems at first sight a genuine clash. One could not have a clearer grouping of parties, and the personal contest does appear this time to spring from an authentic collision of values. Divine law set against human law, family as opposed to state; whatever the precise phrasing one chooses, there would seem at first sight little doubt that in this case two high human principles compete. Yet even here is there a real equivalence of powers? It is to be observed that the play itself has an answer—develops its own view of this question. After sundry false starts and hesitations the feeling of all who matter in the play swings unmistakably against Creon. The Chorus, as usual, have to be wrenched from neutrality, but even the Chorus, when Creon's cause begins to sink, come out strongly and clearly against him: 'We could have told you so' is their cry. Characters with minds of their own leave us in no doubt of their mood. Everyone who counts is for Antigone; everyone who counts, against Creon. There is only one inference from this: the value represented by Creon is suspect. Creon, nominally, is the symbol for state, but if Creon's edict is morally wrong, it cannot stand for a 'justified power'. Creon, in effect, has become detached from the state, is no longer truly its voice. Bradley sums up the gist of the play: 'Antigone has lost her life through her absolute assertion of the family against the state.'[1] But we may make the same criticism as before: one word in the formula is hollow—just a word without any substance. In the case of *Romeo and Juliet* it was 'family'; in the case of this drama it is 'state'.

It is rather interesting to note that in a much inferior drama, the *Heracleidae*, Bradley could have found a much better example of the kind of clash he was thinking of. In this play the claims of the suppliants are truly opposed to the claims of the state. Here a genuine deadlock arises; and only the self-sacrifice of Macaria can end it.

I take another example of what seems to me to be pattern-

[1] *Op. cit.*, p. 74.

31

making from Professor H. D. F. Kitto's *Greek Tragedy*. Mr Kitto has few more interesting and provocative pages than those in which he discusses the greater dramas of Euripides. Mr Kitto sees the problem of those dramas somewhat in this way. Euripides was a very serious and a very able tragedian, yet in the very greatest of his tragedies there are what appear to be peculiar flaws. There is none of them that has not brought forth complaints, or else been buttressed by 'the most desperate apologies'. Yet the paradox of the matter is this, that Euripides could write model plays when he chose; we have only to think of plays like the *Ion* or the *Iphigenia in Tauris* to realize what a deft constructive artist he was. Why is it, then, that in plays intrinsically greater he so often fell short of the standard that in these much lighter plays he attained? Mr Kitto's thesis, in brief, is that the alleged defects of some of these greater tragedies are in a very large measure illusory. It is true that superficially they are imperfect, and that the practice of Sophocles seems against them no less than the theory of Aristotle. But if we look a little more closely at some of these tragedies we shall see what Euripides has in mind. Mr Kitto says we must make a distinction: we must, so to speak, look twice at every major drama of Euripides. We must look first at the visible play—the play that exists in the lines; and then we must look at what is underneath this; what is underneath is a kind of shadow-drama incorporating the 'tragic idea'. The visible play may often seem odd and irregular; it is in the idea that the true shapeliness resides.

Mr Kitto takes the *Medea* for an instance. How few of the rules for great tragedy this drama would seem at first sight to fulfil! Medea is a tragic heroine, but where is her 'tragic flaw'? To try to single out her error would be a laughable and preposterous task. Or take, again, Aristotle's principle of catharsis: what room is there for such a principle here? That impudently triumphant conclusion—how could catharsis possibly arise from this? Mr Kitto recognizes these facts: the quest for the Aristotelian elements would certainly seem hopeless here. But then he proceeds to interpret; bit by bit we are led to a solution. Superficially considered, there can, of course, be no such thing as 'tragic mistake' in this play. But how if the whole existence of Medea is an 'error'—an error, so to speak, of the cosmos itself? Suppose we think of Medea as passion run wild, as something elemental and intrinsic in nature that has reached an exorbitant growth? She herself goes scot free, it is true; but it is not true that nobody pays. She has spread ruin and grief in her wake; in the last analysis it is mankind that suffers—that pays the price (so to say) for Medea. And how can catharsis be saved? Mr Kitto thinks that in an inverted way the very triumph of Medea can provide it. She has outraged the Sun, and what happens? The Sun itself comes to her rescue. It is like the revelation of a horror in nature. It is as if the play is declaring: 'This is what the Universe is like. Do you see what unreason lies at the heart of it, what a monstrous Paradox it is?' And from this glimpse we get a kind of catharsis.

So Mr Kitto discusses the tragedies, allowing everywhere for a sort of dislocation between the *expression* of the drama and the idea. Externally, a tragedy of Euripides may seem to defy all the Aristotelian canons; look beneath, and we shall nearly always see that in a deep way it really conforms. And Mr Kitto approves of the method. He thinks that manipulation of the plot is legitimate, if the dramatist feels that by this process he is serving his tragic idea.

It is obvious that tenets of this kind raise very delicate questions of aesthetic principle. Is a dramatist, we wonder, really justified in playing ducks and drakes with his drama in order that he may bring out more clearly his 'idea'? Are embodiment and idea really separable—can they (dramatically) be kept apart in this way? Is not embodiment the very life and soul of drama, and if we say that a drama does not embody its idea, are we not simply saying that the drama has failed? Can a dramatist manipulate and interfere and still remain a good dramatist? Such questions are, aesthetically, very serious, and it seems to me that the answers that one should give to them would invalidate much of Mr Kitto's discussion. But, apart from the extreme doubtfulness of the theory, one cannot help feeling that Mr Kitto's treatment of these problems puts a very great strain on the plays—that it tends to force them away from themselves into shapes that they do not naturally take. Among the tragedies that Mr Kitto considers is the *Troades*. With Aristotle's theory and Sophocles' practice in mind he sees in the *Troades* 'a play in which no single incident is the "necessary or probable" result of the preceding one, the characterization is slight and inconsistent, the Chorus, far from being a co-actor, takes no notice at all of the action';[1] yet the paradox, which Mr Kitto sees just as clearly, is that the *Troades* is a very great drama indeed. Mr Kitto's discussion of this play is most interesting, but he seems to me to spend disproportionate effort in seeking a *rationale* for its form. We shall not worry about the plot of the *Troades* if

[1] *Greek Tragedy* (1939), p. 192.

we merely realize that it was not meant to have one—that characters were not important for its purpose, and that it was of no consequence whether incidents were linked. This is just another way of saying that the *Troades* is a play *sui generis*, and was never meant to conform to a pattern. To apply Aristotelian theory to the *Troades* is to wreck it, and to plunge ourselves into illimitable confusion. To apply Hegelian theory to it would be worse; but we are under no compulsion to apply any kind of theory to it; we are at liberty to take it as it is and to forget all about patterns of tragedy. And when we look at it with innocent eyes we become aware of its quality in an instant: we may not hit on the happiest phrase for it, but perhaps 'dramatic pageant' will serve. That, at least, is sufficient to place it, and to suggest all the things that it is not. It is not a tragedy, but a tragic spectacle; it has no action (in Aristotle's sense) at all; the conception of plot is irrelevant, and so is every other standard idea about tragedy—except the idea that tragedy is sad. The case of the *Troades* is as simple as this—when we carefully refrain from putting pressure on it or trying to align it with a type.

The case of the *Medea* is not quite so easy. Superficially this play is much closer to the Aristotelian picture of a tragedy; there is an awkward gap, all the same. Mr Kitto acknowledges the gap, but becomes uneasy about it as he continues: he would feel happier if somehow it could be closed. So he works out various ways of restoring to the *Medea* some of the regulation equipment that it lacks. The *Medea*, when Mr Kitto has finished with it, is very nearly orthodox again; it has regained error and catharsis, and could now pass most of the tests.

Mr Kitto's interest in error and catharsis is itself a matter of significance. Nothing reinforces the impulse towards pattern-making like the sanction of a time-honoured dictum. The subject is of sufficient importance to claim a brief chapter to itself.

CHAPTER IV

ARISTOTELIAN DICTA: CATHARSIS

THE difficulties of the *Poetics* are well known. The work belongs to the class of esoteric writings and we seem to be imagining it correctly if we think of it as a set of lecture-notes that would have been expanded and clarified in the utterance. The whole character of the writing suggests this. Aristotle was no stylist, but the treatise shows awkwardnesses and unevennesses and many little peculiarities of composition that can only mean that Aristotle had not fully revised it. In a sense it is at an incomplete stage; it was complete enough for Aristotle's own use of it, but to us it necessarily appears as a basis for what might some day have been rendered complete. The peculiarities of the composition are interesting and have been studied in some detail by scholars.[1] Anyone will be struck by the duplications, by the occasional lapses of memory, the little contradictions and inconsequences. There is, again, the prevailing allusiveness. Examples are given perfunctorily. Aristotle tosses them to us and once or twice has indicated them so tersely that the precise meaning is a little in doubt. There are places where the voice would have helped to bring out the sense of the text, and places where we seem to come upon catchwords—cues and reminders for the speaker. The whole effect is very deceptive.

[1] For example, by Alfred Gudeman in his *Aristoteles Poetik* (1934), pp. 3 ff.

At a first reading nothing could seem much simpler, but with every fresh reading one loses some confidence, and finally one reaches the conviction that no further peering or probing will help. Nearly every sentence is clear, but the paragraphs are not so clear as the sentences, and one becomes less and less sure of the connections. What it means is that in reading the *Poetics* we have to work very hard for ourselves. We are forced to supplement and infer; we have to make little charts of the way Aristotle's mind seems to be moving and then try to trace out the curve of his thought. The difficulty is not usually one of expression, of knowing what the phrases mean. The difficulty is to know what Aristotle is thinking—in what context he is making this assertion, what examples are hovering in his mind as he commits himself to this other. It is very dangerous to take any sentence on its merits, no matter how unequivocal it sounds. The chief rule in reading the *Poetics* is caution: to look carefully before and after, and then to check the meaning of a sentence by what seems to be its background of thought.

Let us try to apply this method to one or two of the famous sayings. What did Aristotle mean by 'error'? Did he mean an error of judgment (that could sometimes be just a blunder)? Or was he thinking of a 'tragic fault'? Only the context will enable us to decide. The first steps in his argument are easy. He is making an assessment of plots and deciding which kinds are unsuitable for tragedy. Three kinds he discards: first, the kind that shows a good man passing from happiness to misery; second, the kind that shows a bad man passing from misery to happiness; third, the kind that shows a bad man passing from happiness to misery. The first kind shocks, the second revolts, the third merely satisfies. Something less extreme is wanted. The best plot has to do with a man who is intermediate in character—not a villain, and yet not out-standingly good—and he must fall through some error. After this Aristotle recapitulates and seeks to drive home his points. He says that the practice of the tragedians confirms him. As the dramatists gained in experience they became more selective in their themes, so that now the finest tragedies are drawn from the stories of just a few houses. He names the following as representative heroes: Alcmeon, Oedipus, Orestes, Meleager, Thyestes, Telephus.

Here, then, is the background of error. Does it provide any clues to the meaning? I think there is one that is nearly decisive—the presence of Thyestes in the list. He does not slip into the argument by oversight; he is mentioned twice in this passage, on the first occasion being paired with Oedipus. How could Aristotle have been thinking of a flaw if at the same time he was thinking of Thyestes? Thyestes was a connoisseur in iniquity, an all-round expert in crime. What would have been the sense of speaking of frailty in connection with a person like this? Mistakes figure largely in his story (as they figure in the story of Oedipus); but as for a tragic flaw—it seems a preposterous thought.

It is in this same passage that Aristotle speaks of Euripides and calls him the 'most tragic' of the poets. What is to be made of this dictum? Euripides can be harsh and uncom-promising, but—most tragic! It is a little surprising.

There is no deep meaning in the dictum. Euripides was being blamed by some critics for making his plays end unhappily, but (says Aristotle) this is nonsense. Tragedies should end unhappily—that is precisely what they are for.

Euripides, therefore, in taking this line is merely observing the spirit of the *genre*. If he has more unhappy endings than other poets that simply makes him 'most tragic'. (Whether he had more is perhaps a question, but presumably that was the impression he made at this time.)

Take, again, the famous saying attributed by Aristotle to Sophocles, that he drew men as they ought to be, Euripides men as they were.[1] It comes in almost as an aside in a discussion of 'truth to fact'. Suppose an artist were drawing an animal and he beautified it a little: gave an extra twirl or two to its horns and removed some unsightly hump; then he could reply, if anyone criticized him, that he was only drawing the animal as it should be. (This is not Aristotle's own instance, but I think it is faithful to his thought.)

The utterance is certainly cryptic, but it would at least seem (from the drift of the passage) that Sophocles was not thinking specifically of goodness but of something like artistic idealization. Did he mean that he made men a little larger than life-size, a little more interesting than they are? (Lear is not 'better' than we are, but he outdoes us in his power of emotion. If we felt ingratitude as we ought to, perhaps we should feel it in the manner of Lear.) Sophocles' greatest characters certainly loom, as those of Euripides do not—and then one remembers Medea and again is assailed by a doubt. On the whole this dictum is not helpful; it would have saved much profitless brain-toil if Aristotle had never reported it, and it is best to dismiss it from the mind.

What, finally, shall we say of catharsis? The basic facts may be set out as follows. There is one mention of catharsis in the *Poetics:* that is where Aristotle defines Tragedy.[2] He

[1] *Poetics*, 1460 b.   [2] *Ibid.*, 1449 b.

says that a tragedy presents an action that is serious and complete in itself; in language with appropriate accompaniments (rhythm, song and so forth); in a dramatic, not a narrative, form; and that it contains incidents that arouse pity and fear, so that the catharsis of those emotions is accomplished. The matter is also raised in the *Politics*, where Aristotle discusses music. People who suffer from 'enthusiasm' can be calmed down and restored to normality by being exposed to emotional music. Aristotle adds that sufferers from other kinds of emotion can be relieved in similar ways. He promises to return to the matter 'when hereafter we speak of poetry'; for the moment he leaves it vague, but later he will speak more precisely. Perhaps he did return to the matter, and perhaps the appropriate pages have been lost. On the other hand it is perhaps rather more likely that when he referred to his work on poetry he was thinking of a different treatise—of one of those *ekdidomenoi logoi*, 'works meant for the general public', of which we have been deprived. The name of such a treatise is known and this may have been the one he was thinking of. But again it is entirely possible that he never wrote his amplification—that reasons, trivial or important, prevented his return to the topic.

As for the crucial sentence itself, there is no real trouble in grasping it. From time to time attempts have been made to show that everything hinges on grammar, but this is the sort of difficulty that arises from too closely staring at anything.[1] The sense is sufficiently clear; and we can go farther

---

[1] See, for example, Anton Bullinger, *Der Endlich Entdeckte Schlüssel zum Verständniss der Aristotelischen Lehre von der Tragischen Katharsis* (1878). Bullinger's thesis is that everything depends on the interpretation of one phrase.

and assert, fairly confidently, that we know the associations of catharsis. Aristotle had in mind the image of 'purging'—there is no reasonable doubt about this. The underlying metaphor is medicinal. He was not thinking of afterglows, of mystic elevations of spirit. (We could be certain of this *a priori:* what did afterglows ever mean to Aristotle, what was a serener light to him?) He was thinking of *purgatio*, not *lustratio*; the process is that of a ridding—an expulsion, a lightening, a relief.

Is there any sense in the notion? It will be useful to halve this question, and to ask first, is there any sense in the notion within Aristotle's own framework of psychology? Then we can ask a second question, is there any sense in it within ours?

One is struck, in modern treatments of catharsis, by the constant emphasis on *tension*. 'He knows that emotion must have an outlet'; 'if people try to bottle up their feelings the accumulated surplus may explode'; 'tragedy is a sort of nervous specific which provides a "good clearance" of emotion'; 'people who void their hysterics by reading accounts of racing . . . might better turn to the "aperient" of Greek drama'[1]: this is a typical handful of comments. At first glance they seem to make sense, but then we remember what is under discussion: not some morbid condition of the nerves but the well-known emotions of pity and fear. These emotions, as we ordinarily think of them, do not call in any marked way for unbottling. In what sense can the pitiful or the fearful be said to be in need of an outlet? One would have said that the emotions of such people had too much

[1] W. Hamilton Fyfe, introduction to *Aristotle's Art of Poetry* (1940), pp. xvi ff.

outlet already. Why should we think that a course of tragedy should be of benefit to the excessively nervous? Above all, why should people who have these emotions be thought of as in a condition of *stress*—as suffering from the sort of 'disquietude' that 'arises from an unsatisfied want'?[1] This seems to be the recurrent confusion. Such discussions assume that a theatre-goer is a person on the brink of hysteria; and the analogies that are brought forward to enlighten us usually rest on a similar assumption. We are told that primitive peoples find it hard to control their emotions; joy or sorrow is to them rather devastating until it has expressed itself in the dance. But we, as we queue up for our tickets, are not necessarily fresh from a joy or heavy-laden with sorrow.

So far I have been talking of these matters on what may be termed the commonsense level; but what is important to observe is that this is Aristotle's own level. Pity and fear figure in his psychological framework as they do in our ordinary parlance; he has no special theory of their nature. Fear is the pain or disturbance due to the image of some threatening evil.[2] Pity is exactly the emotion that we ourselves understand by the word.[3] Aristotle discusses them both in his shrewd and practical way. On the commonsense view of emotion, how can pity and fear be cravings, or states of stress requiring relief?

There is, of course, another view of these matters.[4] It would seem that fear works obliquely; that many things of

---

[1] Ingram Bywater, *Aristotle on the Art of Poetry* (1909), pp. 155-6.

[2] *Rhetoric*, 1382 a.

[3] *Ibid.*, 1385 b.

[4] I have received much help hereabouts from talks with my friend Professor W. M. O'Neil.

which we are afraid are in reality serving us as substitutes for other things too dreadful to face. If our fear is cut off in one direction it can find a way out in another. The objects of which we are frightened may not really warrant the response; we may be using them to get rid of emotions that for some reason are suffering a blockage—to take the edge off an inner tension that is pressing hard for relief. In this way drama may be helpful, for obviously it teems with material well adapted to the releasing of tension. And when we use the drama to release our tensions perhaps we may be said to be obtaining catharsis.

But let us not think that when we have taken all this into account we have solved the problem of catharsis. In a way, we have proved too much—are now, in fact, so far beyond the original idea that little of profit is left. Of one thing we can be quite certain: we are no longer in possession of a *test*. Aristotle wrote of catharsis almost as if it were a criterion of tragedy, as if this were what it led up to and were one of the chief signs by which we should know it. And that is the way Milton understood him: 'Tragedy, as it was antiently compos'd, hath been ever held the gravest, moralest, and most profitable of all other Poems: therefore said by *Aristotle* to be of power by raising pity and fear, or terror, to purge the mind of those and such like passions, that is to temper and reduce them to just measure with a kind of delight, stirr'd up by reading or seeing those passions well imitated.'[1] 'The most profitable of all other Poems': tragedy can enjoy no such pride of place in any modern theory of catharsis. If the processes I have described mean catharsis,

---

[1] *Samson Agonistes* (1671), 'Of that sort of Dramatic Poem which is called Tragedy'.

then catharsis is exactly where you find it. The children who gibber at Tarzan, the addicts of the strip-tease—all are enjoying catharsis, and one catharsis is as good as another. And minor perplexities arise. For example, there is the question of dosage. Presumably, those who stand to gain most from a drama are those who are most tightly wound—whose inner reserve stock of tension is nearly at the bursting point. The ideal audience for (say) the *Medea* would presumably be an audience of neurotics. In this sense there is a premium on morbidity. But the dose could perhaps be too strong—the whole situation is full of surmise. Or suppose that a person were normal (or as close as one may get to that state); then he would be out of luck at the theatre, for he would not qualify for catharsis at all. One can imagine an audience that was hand-picked—only a committee of psychologists could choose it—so as to contain just the right amount of collective frustration to give it full value from a drama. I would suggest that these absurdities are intrinsic to any modern theory of catharsis.

How Aristotle developed his theory it is idle even to attempt to imagine. His root difficulty would have been to bring pity and fear (as he thought of them) into line with enthusiasm and frenzy. The theory seems to be a theory of repressions, so far as it is clarified at all. The one clear thing in the whole matter is enthusiasm, and the means by which this morbid condition is relieved. This is something that Aristotle has seen—perhaps it was the starting point of his thought. And did he perceive in his doctrine of catharsis a way of replying to Plato? Plato had written of the *good* of music in ministering to abnormal states; but he had spoken of the *harm* of tragedy in exciting pity and fear. Aristotle's treatise is a silent protest against Plato's whole attitude to drama. Did it occur to him that in homoeopathy he had a particularly neat reply? If he could link pity and fear with frenzy, then he could beat Plato on Plato's own ground. Wild music drives out wildness; could fear also drive out fear? If that was a legitimate hypothesis it would be a perfect answer to Plato, for in that case tragedy would be justified by the doctrines of Plato himself.

If that was really the way of it, it was certainly a neat riposte. But perhaps also it was a little impetuous. As Aristotle pressed more closely on his theory in analysis did he find it dwindling away?

PART II

THE PLAYS AND THEIR PROBLEMS

CHAPTER V

'DIPTYCH' PLAYS: THE *AJAX*

I IMAGINE that readers coming rather late to the study of Greek drama (and bringing with them some experience of other literature) must often be a little surprised, perhaps puzzled, by one of its characteristics. They will be prepared to find that Greek dramatists—because of the nature of the Greek theatre, because of Greek dramatic convention—had their special problems; they will hardly be prepared to find that one of the most insistent of these problems was the problem of unity itself. Yet to all appearance it was so.

There are faint anticipatory signs of the problem even in Aeschylus, though his special methods keep it very firmly in check; but there is, for an example, a faint foreshadowing of it in the last hundred lines of the *Agamemnon*. The theme of those lines is the feud between Aegisthus and the representatives of the city. It can be asserted, in defence, that in these lines we have the preparation for the second play of the trilogy, but I doubt the sufficiency of this answer. Perhaps it was important that towards the end of the first play we should be given a preliminary sight of Aegisthus; all the same that final sequence constitutes rather a pendant to the theme of the *Agamemnon* than an anticipation of the theme of the *Choephoroe*.

Turn, for instance, to what Mr Kitto has to say of the *Agamemnon*. His pages on it are among his most interesting.

But then, when one has laid down his book one is struck, on reflection, by a curious fact: the final sequence of the play has had not even a mention. I think that is quite significant. A critic like Mr Kitto—alert, sympathetic, appreciative—does not find room in his discussion of the *Agamemnon* for its last hundred lines, although the development they present is so new and arresting. Intent on putting the *Agamemnon* through its paces he instinctively ignores those lines, not because in any sense they are a disgrace to Aeschylus—far from it—but because he recognizes unconsciously that they have no true part in the design of the play. I would suggest, myself, that in these final lines of the *Agamemnon* what we are really perceiving is a 'diptych' in process of emergence.

I am not sure whether it was Professor Webster or an earlier scholar who first brought this term into currency. It saves periphrases and is a useful figure of speech for a play with a twofold construction; and 'diptychs', of course, are the plays that exemplify the difficulty I have spoken of—that slight but insistent trouble with unity that is so curious a feature of Greek drama. Aeschylus had his own automatic solutions, but with the other two dramatists the trouble seems real.

Every diptych, needless to say, has had its apologists. The apologists usually urge us to find the right point of view: they say that once that is found the difficulties will fade, the doubleness will be seen as illusory, the theme will appear as essentially single after all. I do not feel, for my own part, that these defences succeed. I think that diptychs exist, that in such plays a division of interest does really occur, and that because of this some power ebbs away from the drama.

Let us consider an example or two. There is the *Ajax* itself.

Ajax dies at a point considerably short of two-thirds of the way through the drama: for the rest of the time the issue of his burial is debated. From this short statement alone one could almost predict the result. It would be a miracle if the interest did not diminish, if the tension did not, in some measure, go flat. I do not think that there can be any question that this has been, in fact, the result. It is not simply that we ourselves, as modern readers, have a much less pressing interest in the matter—that burial-rites are less important for us than for Greeks. It is very easy for us to regain imaginatively a sense of their importance. But the earliest readers of this play felt about it, as far as we can judge, almost exactly as we do: they were a little puzzled by its peculiar construction, wondered why Sophocles had so extended his theme, and thought (whatever his reason) that in doing so he had somewhat weakened his play.

Take, again, the *Hippolytus*. This is a most striking play with passage after passage in Euripides' most pregnant vein. But it is difficult to defend its structure. As in the *Ajax*, the facts almost speak for themselves. Phaedra drops out at the half-way point. Critics hasten to remind us that the play is called *Hippolytus* and not *Phaedra*, but the title makes very little difference to the facts. The true drama of this play is bound up with Phaedra—no 'inner meaning', no 'thesis' that we may care to extract, changes that. With her departure goes all the interest of a genuine conflict, for nothing comparable remains. Hippolytus struggles slightly with himself —whether he shall or shall not tell the truth—but this is a meagre emotional trouble indeed when put against the agonizing torments that have been Phaedra's. Further, the punishment that falls on Hippolytus is external. In principle, it is exactly the same as if he had had a fatal accident one day while out hunting, and the goddess had said: 'Take that! That is your reward for rejecting Love.' He is not punished, that is to say, in and through his priggishness (as Sir Willoughby Patterne is punished in and through his egoism), not reached in his essential self. And perhaps this is why one cannot but feel that the *Hippolytus*, for all its charm, is something of a light-weight amongst tragedies. But how the lack of dramatic force in the young man's fate sharpens our sense of all that we have lost by the early going of Phaedra! With her goes the true life of the play.

Or consider—an even more interesting case—the *Antigone;* it is more interesting because the doubleness is subtler, because the break is not nearly so sharp. What we have in the *Antigone* is an imperceptible glide—a hidden shift from one theme to another. In the earlier parts of the play it is, of course, Antigone herself who attracts and rivets our attention: she is, and she remains, by far the most interesting character in the drama. She is the character who initiates, who does the startling and unusual thing; Creon is commonplace by comparison. During all the first third of the action there is hardly a question in our minds that the drama is chiefly about her—that she is the person who matters. Creon is interesting enough in his way, but not in her fresh and original way. He is negative to her positive, he reacts where she acts, he simply takes up a stubborn position and sticks to it, and because of his stubbornness he begins presently to meet with reverses. All this has an interest, but nothing to compare with the interest of what Antigone does, of the stand she takes. Then, after a while, she begins to lose ground in the drama; presently she is no longer at its centre.

Then she drops out, and we are left with Creon about to face the consequences of his sin. This has its effectiveness, it is true, but the drama has changed by now. Let us compare it with *King Lear* or *Macbeth*. We travel a long road in *Macbeth*, and we lose Lady Macbeth in the course of the journey; but at the end of *Macbeth* we have no doubt whatever that we are still within the play with which we started. So it is with *Lear*. We travel a long long way in *Lear*, but at the finish we are still within the drama *King Lear*. Our sensation in the *Antigone* is different. The *Antigone* is a much shorter play than either of these others, but in the *Antigone* the road, in a sense, is longer, and by the time we have reached the end of this road the beginning is no longer in sight. There is no exaggeration—none whatever—in saying that Antigone is forgotten in the last hundred lines or so of her play. She has become by this time incidental to what is now exclusively a tragedy of Creon; and Creon himself is being punished, not specifically for what he did to Antigone, but because, though well-intentioned, he was blind and stubborn and proud. The entry of Eurydice, so close to the finish, helps to show how far from Antigone we have drawn.

But why, it may be asked, should the centre of equilibrium not shift? Is there a law that forbids it to move on in this way? Is not a dramatist entitled to adopt the double construction if he likes it? Suppose a play does start with one character in the foreground and finish with another in that place, is there anything that prohibits such procedure—does it matter? It does matter, and Somerset Maugham in the following sentence (penned with no thought of Greek drama in mind) has explained to us why: 'It is a psychological trait in human nature that interest is established in persons whom the playwright introduces at the beginning of his play so firmly that if the interest is then switched off to other persons who enter the scene later a sense of disappointment ensues.'[1] The principle at the heart of this dictum is, without any question, one of the most important of all the principles that apply to the writing of fiction; it is, I suppose, the most important of them all; and it is ignored by an exponent of the craft (whether he deals in novels, in dramas, or in epics) at his peril. Maugham's statement, modified slightly this way or that, has a relevance to each of the plays just discussed: in each of them, however great the initial power, there is occasion before the finish for some slight sense of disappointment.

Let us now glance briefly at statistics. Of the seven plays of Sophocles that survive two are diptychs; a third, the *Antigone*, is not an outright diptych but in a milder way shows somewhat the same peculiarity of structure. Of the serious plays of Euripides seventeen or eighteen survive; of these, four at least are diptychs (one, the *Heracles*, can with some reason be accounted a triptych). These four include two (the *Hecuba* and the *Andromache*) of an inferior cast, but also two (the *Heracles* and the *Hippolytus*) that are deservedly among the most celebrated plays of Euripides.

[1] *The Summing Up* (1938), p.122. This was one of the reasons (there are many others) for the crash of Henry James' *Guy Domville*: 'With the next act [the second] came a change. The author had done a dangerous thing in dropping most of the first-act characters and introducing a new set in whom little interest was taken. The excellence of the opening was now a draw-back, the audience wanted more of it; they longed to follow the fortunes of Marion Terry and sulkily refused to be interested in the doings of Miss Millard'—just as we (or most of us) sulkily refuse to be interested in Menelaus. (W. Graham Robertson, quoted by S. Nowell-Smith in *The Legend of the Master* [1947], p. 64).

It seems fair to assume that among the plays of either dramatist that are now dark to us there must have been additional
examples, and indeed it is quite certain, from the evidence
we have, that there were. Of the lost plays of Sophocles
these four at least must have taken the form: *Assembly of
Achaeans*, *Epigoni*, *Odysseus Acanthoplex*, *Tereus*.[1] Among
the lost Euripidean dramas it seems likely that the *Chrysippus*
took the diptych shape, and I think it is evident that the
Phaethon was also of the form—the play that Goethe so
wished he could have read. The fragments suggest that
Phaethon disappeared from the scene some time before the
finish (near the two-thirds mark, it would seem); what
happened after that is not known.

We have a right to draw inferences from these facts,
limited and incomplete though they are. We may argue,
indeed, somewhat after the fashion of astronomers who
assume that the disposition of the stars they can see will be
repeated in the spaces that are beyond their ken. Of the
plays of these two dramatists that we have, seven take the
diptych form; and this is a conservative count. Of the plays
that are lost, but that we are in a position to make conjec-
tures about, six would appear to have been of a similar build
(and this, again, is a guarded estimate). Risking a figure, it
would seem not unreasonable to suppose that between them
the two dramatists wrote about twenty plays of the diptych
form: in other words, that about one in ten of their plays
took this shape.

The proportion is high, and must surely be significant of
something. It is not quite possible to write off the diptych
plays as exceptions: the suggestion is rather of a drift. It is

[1] See T. B. L. Webster, *An Introduction to Sophocles* (1936), pp. 172 ff.

as if Greek drama has a bias, as if there are conditions that impel it towards this patterning. I think that there are such conditions and that it is possible to some extent to define them.

Let us consider *Macbeth*. For a Shakespearian tragedy *Macbeth* is very tight and spare in its build, and the theme is one that could have had considerable appeal for the Greeks. It is interesting to reflect on the kind of play that *Macbeth* would have been if from its make-up three kinds of dramatic stuff could have been excluded: first, very violent and exciting action; second, scenes that depend on a group; third, developments of a subsidiary or collateral kind. The results of this imaginary revision are surprising. Large sections of the drama immediately disappear. Nearly the whole of the fifth act must go, for the action here is of a wild and clanging sort that Greek taste could not have borne for a moment. But not only that: it is possible that the very central scene would go, for the words of Macbeth and Lady Macbeth when Duncan has been murdered within are in themselves so excited and tense—so urgent and active in their nature—that it is doubtful whether Greek drama could have stood them: the colloquy having in itself so much of the condition of violent and exciting action. The scene of the discovery must also go, for this is a scene that depends on a group. The principle here seems interesting. If one lets one's mind rove quickly over some assorted scenes of Shakespeare that one has found very gripping, one realizes that a surprisingly large number of them derive their force from a group. It is not merely that the sheer fact of the company of people engaged brings a variety of interests to a focus; it is rather that some mysterious force is *generated* by the group—a quality of emotion that without it could not have come into being. *King Lear*, for example, reaches its climax with the great 'O reason not the need!', the speech that finishes with the broken cry, 'O fool, I shall go mad'. But that speech is possible only because Lear has been standing in the middle of a group. It would not have been possible if he had been arguing with Regan alone. It is necessary that Goneril should have arrived on the scene, that Kent and Cornwall and the Fool should be there, and that they should not be just standers-by. It is the friction of all these personalities together that generates the drama of the scene. So, at a slightly lower level, with the discovery scene in *Macbeth*. Lady Macbeth faints when she hears the slain Duncan described; but it would have been very different if she had been talking alone with Macbeth. She faints because she is one of a company, and because the eyes and deep breaths of the company convey to her a horror that she has not yet felt for herself.

In a Greek drama the two critical scenes at the heart of *Macbeth* would have been compressed into a messenger's speech. (There are messenger elements, of course, in *Macbeth*; Macbeth himself acts as messenger for ten lines or so of this same discovery scene.) In the Greek play that might have been the counterpart of *Macbeth* the messenger's speech would, without question, have been a wonderful thing; but the quantitative difference is clear. There are other group scenes in *Macbeth*, some of them of hardly less importance than this (the banquet scene is one); and apart from group scenes there are scenes that allow some collateral action to develop. Scenes of this kind are surprisingly numerous. One thinks of *Macbeth* as of a compact play, very swift in its movement; and of course it is, in truth, such a play. Nevertheless, there are many accompaniments to the action, and a number of scenes that might quite fairly receive the name of diversions. A short scene of this class is the famous porter's speech; a longer one is the fourth scene of the second act, where Ross and the old man talk about the weather and are presently joined by Macduff. There are few irrelevancies in the play, but there are many subsidiary actions of lesser or greater interest that support the principal theme. And they not only support it: they keep it for long stretches in a state of suspension. Subtract these subsidiary scenes, take away also the group scenes and the scenes of visible and violent action, and I estimate that *Macbeth* would collapse to about a quarter of its present size.

I think that these considerations throw some real light on the leaning of Greek drama towards the diptych. The exclusions I have listed are drastic; it is a little difficult, in such a convention, to spin out a theme—and 'spin out' need not connote a merely trivial process. By the group, as I have suggested, a certain kind of action is spun: a precious texture of drama that only a company of actors together can weave. So it is with those other resources that the Greek dramatist could never employ. We need not for a moment repine; no one thinks of the Greek playwright as handicapped, no one regards him as frustrated. All the same, he contends, I think, with a certain difficulty that would leave an Elizabethan or a modern dramatist untouched. It is a little harder for him to *brake* his play, to keep it from moving ahead too fast. Every play begins with what may be called an initial charge, and the problem for the dramatist is to control it. In a Greek drama this initial charge is always in danger of spending itself a little too soon; to husband that charge is for the Greek dramatist the problem of problems. The problem sometimes defeats him, and then there is really only one measure he can take. He must reinforce the exhausted charge: that means, in other words, that he must inject, before the play has run out, a new charge: in effect, that he must turn his play into a diptych.

Again, a Greek drama is straitly channelled; because of its conventions its movement is along a narrow track and it cannot diverge from this track. An Elizabethan drama can proceed by expansions; as it goes along it can gather new people to itself, and up to a point it can hold them. It can throw out branches, exploit side issues, and indulge in skirmishings off the direct path of its progress. A Greek drama is not capable of these deployments, nor can a Greek drama grow by accretion. Its personnel is strictly limited, and throughout the whole course of the action must remain so. This means, in effect, that an addition is almost necessarily followed by a subtraction. If an important new character comes in there ensues a kind of competitive pressure for place. Because the track is narrow and the walls of the play, so to speak, are rigid, the belated incoming of any character of note puts a severe tax on the available room: what happens as a rule is that some other character, already in the play, is squeezed out. The *Hippolytus* itself exemplifies this process. It is not modern sentiment, merely, that causes us to regret the early departure of Phaedra; her departure is to be regretted for the strictest dramatic reasons —for reasons that always had force; it is a pity, on every count, that she should leave the play so soon. In a modern play there would be no question of her going; and it is for this reason, above all, that she has to go from the Greek play: that a Greek play is not able to cope with a set of three people who are at once so important and so closely involved as Theseus and Hippolytus and Phaedra. For she could hardly have remained in the drama except at the price of a strong triangular clash, and that is a price that Greek drama is not prepared to pay. Greek drama has a number of examples to show of the mildly triangular scene, but it never overcame its distaste for the full-blooded triangular clash.

It is instructive to compare Racine. He, of course, wanted to retain his Phèdre—was not at all interested in a type of treatment that would jettison her half-way through. On the other hand he too, in this particular instance, was disinclined for the risks of a poignant triangular scene. He has it easily both ways. He keeps Phèdre as long as he wishes: keeps her till but ten lines of the play remain to be spoken; yet not once do his three principals meet. They weave in and out, they come together two by two, but the three of them never collide. In Greek drama this would have been an impossible feat. Racine can accomplish it because he has more room in his drama for manoeuvre; and this again depends on the vital fact that he can allow himself an ampler personnel to deploy. He has ways of keeping his principals occupied, he can, so to speak, draw them off—to Aricie, the confidant, the Nurse. (There are few more fascinating studies in the tactics of playwriting than to watch what Racine does with Aricie.) Euripides did not possess this resource: there were no means by which he could have kept his principals dispersed; so his heroine has to go, and with her goes the true dramatic *vis* of his play.

A good deal, then, will depend upon subject-matter. The impact of the theme, in Greek drama, is relatively direct and 'uncushioned'. There are many themes, needless to say, that cause not the slightest trouble, that meet the requirements of Greek drama exactly. There are also some special cases, some stories of peculiar build, that seem as if made for the uses of Greek dramatists: the example of examples is the story of Oedipus. And of course, whatever the theme, the difficulties that I have spoken of are again and again surmounted. It is important merely to note that they exist and that sometimes their effects become visible.

Every diptych, as I say, has its defenders, and the *Ajax* is no exception to this rule. Professor Bowra, for instance, feels that we have dealt sufficiently with the problem of its structure when we have recognized that Sophocles had two themes in mind. There is, first, the ruin of Ajax; next, there is the rehabilitation of his character after death. We have to see why Ajax falls, and, after that, why he is rightly honoured. This, certainly, gives a simplified *description* of the play, but I do not think that it brings us very much nearer to an explanation or justification of its structure. We understand well that it was essential to Sophocles' plan to bring out the inherent worth of his hero. But then he has gone a very long way towards accomplishing this before the first part of the play is over. It would have been a very dull spectator who, called away from the theatre at the point where the hero dies, had failed to take with him a strong impression that Ajax was noble. No man could have suffered as we have seen Ajax suffer—no man, after disgrace, could have acted as Ajax acted—without possessing intrinsic greatness of soul; and it is very much the business of a dramatist, in cases of this kind, to show the greatness and the wrong-doing together. *Othello* rests on a somewhat similar combination of themes, but Shakespeare does not feel obliged to wait until his main action is over before he proceeds to the task of rehabilitating his hero; nor is it necessary, for this rehabilitation, that we should have a set discussion of the merits and defects of Othello. The rehabilitation is automatic; it comes from all that we have learnt of Othello through the course of the drama. It is not altogether unlike this with Ajax. I doubt whether the later section of the play tells us one important thing about Ajax that we do not already know for ourselves. We glean a few more details of his prowess: but it can hardly be said that these are required; for if one assumption of the play is more basic than another it is that Ajax is a mighty man of war. We learn of the great esteem that in some quarters he has won, of the loyalty that he has been able to inspire; and all this is instructive in its way. But the dominant fact is the shift in the interest. The question whether Ajax is to receive honourable burial is not, in strict accuracy, a question about Ajax; we have already made up our minds about Ajax. It is a question about the men who debate—about Odysseus and Menelaus and Agamemnon. Our attention is drawn away, insensibly, from the topic of the argument to the arguers; so far as we are held at all, it is the clash of the personalities that holds us. Critics remind us that Ajax still remains in our view, and much is made of the effect of this tableau. But it is not in human nature to hold a tableau in gaze while a live wrangle competes for attention. And the wrangle takes in so many issues—makes for so many forays into politics and ethics—that Ajax is edged still farther from the centre of interest. As for the rehabilitation itself, when all is said it is partial only, an inconclusive and formal matter, an agreement that on one side is quite insincere. Agamemnon consents to it as a favour to Odysseus; as far as he and Menelaus are concerned Ajax remains precisely the villain he always was.

Then there is the question of the Athenian audience and what this audience would have expected of the play: many critics have thought that the secret of the matter lies here. Mr Bowra himself takes this view. The honour of Ajax was of deep concern to Athenians, for Athenians had a vested interest in Ajax. Their feeling, as Jebb suggested, would have been 'analogous to that of a medieval audience witnessing a drama which concerned the life of a canonized saint'[1]: and even a little more than that, for the fortunes of this man were intertwined with their own traditions. All such considerations are important, but it is essential that we should note their bearing: they are important as *motives* for the play; they help us to understand, perhaps, how its structure came about; they have no validity whatever as justifying this structure. Nor does it advance us much to try to readjust our viewpoint and to think of the play as about Ajax's death. That is the real theme, it is sometimes said; ancient readers themselves perceived it when they called the play 'Death of Ajax'. But this is not much more than an ingenious evasion: it merely steps round the facts. Are we to sum up the whole first part of the drama as being 'what was preparatory to Ajax's death'? This is to reduce the action to an absurdity. The earlier scenes of the *Ajax* are full of the most gripping event: the slaughter of the cattle, the intervention of the

[1] *Sophocles: The Ajax* (1896), p. xxxii.

goddess, the horror and shame of the madness, the wild fluctuations of emotion in Ajax, his rage, his humiliation, his bitterness: all these are dramatic realities with the most vivid interest of their own. Surely we are not to be called upon, in order that some theory of the play may be served, to bundle all these scenes together as 'what came before Ajax's death'.

Mr Kitto has another solution. He suggests that the key to the play is Odysseus—that it is Odysseus who makes it a unity. The play begins and ends with Odysseus, and his importance in general, Mr Kitto thinks, has been much undervalued. 'In the prologue the most striking thing, even more striking than the appearance of Ajax mad, is Odysseus' attitude to him. . . . He is, if not as prominent as the hero Ajax, at least as essential to the play, much more essential than Teucer.' In his own person, he 'attains moral grandeur'.[1] Mr Kitto, I think, has stared too hard and too closely at Odysseus and has ended by getting him quite out of focus. One of Mr Kitto's assertions about Odysseus has point: we could not very well spare him from the play—could spare him perhaps less easily than Teucer. The other assertions seem to me to be false: they throw the facts of the play quite out of perspective. We are interested in the attitude of Odysseus to Ajax, but how can this possibly affect us more forcibly than the spectacle of Ajax himself in his madness? Again, is it not to exaggerate rather absurdly to declare that Odysseus is as essential to the drama as Ajax? Is it even true to say of him, as Mr Kitto does, that 'he is kept prominently before our notice'? From the time of his exit to the time of his re-entry there are half a dozen or so references to Odysseus. Every such reference is brief; not one of them is

[1] *Op. cit.*, pp. 121-2.

of much importance; most merely say things about him that we already know or could easily guess. Only twice is he mentioned by Ajax, each time in connection with the Atreidae. In the two final speeches of Ajax—two of the most important speeches in the play—Odysseus receives no notice at all, though in both of these the Atreidae are prominent. If we are to go by force and frequency of allusion, it is the Atreidae who obsess the mind of Ajax, it is upon them that he chiefly broods. The truth surely is that in that long interval of his absence Odysseus is very seldom in our minds. As for the personal impression he makes, does not 'moral grandeur' overstate it? Is not the pitch of that phrase rather high? He is a notable foil to Ajax, and very interesting as a character in his wisdom, his calm, his detachment. But nothing of this quite suffices to make him joint-pillar of the play with Ajax; that seems an exorbitant claim. That would be like putting Horatio on a level with Hamlet, or according Banquo a half-share in *Macbeth*.

We cannot enter the mind of Sophocles, and we shall never know just why he chose to build the *Ajax* as he did. The problem of the twofold construction is especially puzzling here, because in this case at least there was no obvious need for the pattern. As we have noticed, it is not at all difficult to see why some plays fall into the diptych shape: they are almost pushed into it by their topics. But that is not the situation here. There was nothing in the Ajax story that required a design like this. Why did not Sophocles choose to start at a point farther back in the story? That would have brought the climax of the play into a later—and really more suitable—position; and there would still have been a chance to give due attention to the burial of Ajax.

For it is a point to be noted, I think, that Sophocles is not exactly pressed for time in the latter portion of the drama. The impression is rather different: really, that he has more time than he quite knows what to do with. Menelaus theorizes abstractly, and his theories take him far from the point; nor, granting the taste of the time for wit-combats, was there any special reason for indulging that taste just here. The later part of the play is longer than need be: the treatment is not at all concise.

We shall never know the answer to the riddle; I would merely suggest that it might have been a simpler answer than we are sometimes inclined to think. The evidence of the fragments is sometimes revealing. There is that lost play of Sophocles with the alternative titles, *Niptra*, *Odysseus Acanthoplex*; presumably the titles are alternative; in naming it the grammarians apparently followed their personal taste. There must have been two quite distinct parts to this play. In the first part of it Odysseus returned and was recognized by his old servant as she washed him; in the second an oracle was fulfilled, and Odysseus received a fatal wound at the hands of Telegonus, his own son. There is a strong suggestion here of deliberate choice—no suggestion of *avoiding* a diptych. On the contrary, it is almost as if Sophocles has gone out of his way to commit one; and perhaps there was something typical in this. It may be that the Greek dramatists outgrew their diptychs; the evidence, on the whole, would seem to suggest that they did. But certainly in their earlier phases they would appear to have struggled but feebly against them. Let us imagine a case like this: a legend (as it might be of Odysseus or Ajax) that fell into a succession of 'lengths'; and between four of these lengths (call them 1, 2, 3, 4) let us imagine this sort of relation: between 1 and 2, and between 3 and 4, very close causal connections, but between 2 and 3 a very definite break in the sequence. Suppose a Greek dramatist to be looking this legend over for material. It would not be at all surprising to find him making for parts 2 and 3 and (in contravention of all canons of unity) proceeding to put them together in a play. There is very little doubt that this in fact is what he would have done if it had happened that those parts interested him more than part 1 and part 4. And, at bottom, it could have been in some such way as this that the *Ajax* came to be built as it is.

The problem of the genesis will never be solved, but the critical problem is easy: the twofold construction weakens the play. The scholiast saw that truth and summed it up once for all: Sophocles, by prolonging the drama, allowed the tragic feeling to evaporate, let the tension of his play go slack.

Before leaving the play let us look at one problem of detail: of its kind there is no more interesting problem in Sophocles, and it raises very important principles of interpretation.

After Ajax has recovered from his madness the course that the play will take seems predictable. The mood of Ajax himself sets steadily in one direction. His life is now a spoiled and broken thing, and there is nothing that he can do to repair it. It becomes clear to him that only one deed remains, a deed by which he may at least confer a parting dignity on his disgraced and shattered existence. This, of course, is to bring his life to a swift finish. His hates, his shames, his despairs all crystallize into this decision. No overt word is spoken, but between the lines of what everyone says we can read the general fear; everyone around Ajax seems to see what is coming. His wife pleads with him not to forsake her; his friends, the sailors, are deeply disturbed. His own behaviour becomes more and more ominous. He commands that his little son be brought—is angrily insistent when Tecmessa seems to demur—and addresses to him what seems like a veiled goodbye. He says that there will be no cause to fear, that he is entrusting him to the care of Teucer. He makes then what seems like a last bequest to the child, bidding him take the broad shield after which he is named. Then, having set his affairs to rights, he peremptorily orders the doors to be closed. We can only conclude (as his wife and his friends conclude) that he means to take his life forthwith.

Instead, to the astonishment of the Chorus, Tecmessa and ourselves, he re-enters a few moments later in what seems an entirely different mood; indeed, he is to all appearance a changed man. He begins a speech of thoughtful and sombre beauty. The feeling of it is so deep that we are compelled to believe that he means what he says. He says that Tecmessa has won. For the pity of her and the child he finds that he cannot carry through his purpose. He is going now to the shore to cleanse himself of his stains and to bury the sword of Hector. He will submit, after all, to the gods and will learn to reverence the Atreidae. What he seems to be saying, in short, is that he is about to make a new start in life—that he is sweeping the past away. This is the meaning that we are obliged to take, precisely as Ajax's friends are obliged to take it. Only in the last ten lines of the speech can we detect a faintly ominous note. He sounds here as if he is about to go on a very long journey indeed—much farther than just to the beach. He sounds, in fact, as if once again he is bidding farewell. Yet the clues, if they exist, are faint; the tenor of the speech seems clear. Here it is, in Jebb's translation.

All things the long and countless years first draw from darkness, then bury from light; and there is nothing for which man may not look; the dread oath is vanquished, and the stubborn will. For even I, erst so wondrous firm—yea, as iron hardened in the dipping,—felt the keen edge of my temper softened by yon woman's words; and I feel the pity of leaving her a widow with my foes, and the boy an orphan.

But I will go to the bathing-place and the meadows by the shore, that in purging of my stains I may flee the heavy anger of the goddess. Then I will seek out some untrodden spot, and bury this sword, hatefullest of weapons, digging in the earth where none shall see; no, let Night and Hades keep it underground! For since my hand took this gift from Hector, my worst foe, to this hour I have had no good from the Greeks. Yes, men's proverb is true: *The gifts of enemies are no gifts, and bring no good.*

Therefore, henceforth I shall know how to yield to the gods, and learn to revere the Atreidae. They are rulers, so we must submit. How else? Dread things and things most potent bow to office; thus it is that snow-strewn winter gives place to fruitful summer; and thus night's weary round makes room for day with her white steeds to kindle light; and the breath of dreadful winds can allow the groaning sea to slumber; and, like the rest, almighty Sleep looses whom he has bound, nor holds with a perpetual grasp.

And we—must we not learn discretion? I, at least, will learn it; for I am newly aware that our enemy is to be hated but as one who will hereafter be a friend; and towards a friend I would wish but thus far to show aid and service, as knowing that he will not always abide. For to most men the haven of friendship is false.

But concerning these things it will be well. Woman, go thou

within, and pray to the gods that in all fulness the desires of my heart may be fulfilled. And ye, my friends, honour ye these my wishes even as she doth; and bid Teucer, when he comes, have care for me, and good-will towards you withal. For I will go whither I must pass; but do ye what I bid; and ere long, perchance, though now I suffer, ye will hear that I have found peace.[1]

There are some observations to make on this speech. First, we must admit, I think, that the general effect of it is quite overpowering—its *tenor* is beyond all mistaking. There are those explicit declarations of intent: he is going to dig a hole and bury his sword, he has decided to alter his whole attitude towards the Atreidae, he will change his philosophy of life. We have to imagine, as we listen to this speech, that we are responding freshly—that we are hearing a first performance of the play. We have no clear notion, as yet, of the sequel. We have *some* notion, of course, of what is to come, but we do not know the exact course of the drama. The speech will greatly surprise us, but we shall simply not be in a position, at this point, to question it. The final verses will perhaps strike us as strange: they will make us wonder a little, perhaps doubt, perhaps even suspect. But we have no leisure to *work out* the matter. The lines can hardly do more than leave us slightly bewildered: they cannot—set against those so positive, so definite assertions—bring home to us an inner intention. And it would be difficult even for our incipient doubts to stand against the joyous outburst of the chorus which follows:

The destroying god hath lifted the cloud of dread trouble from our eyes. Joy, joy! Now, once again, now, O Zeus, can the pure brightness of good days come to the swift sea-cleaving

[1] Vv. 646-92, trans. Jebb (revised ed. 1907).

ships: since Ajax again forgets his trouble, and hath turned to perform the law of the gods with all due rites, in perfectness of loyal worship.

The strong years make all things fade; nor would I say that aught was too strange for belief, when thus, beyond our hopes, Ajax hath been led to repent of his wrath against the Atreidae, and his dread feuds.[1]

It is to be repeated that at this point of the drama we *must* share the feelings of the Chorus and Tecmessa about Ajax, precisely as the original spectators of the drama would have shared them. It is of no consequence that the general outline of the legend was known and that Sophocles would have been expected almost certainly to follow it. We do not yet know what the precise track of the play is to be—we know nothing of the wheres and the whens and the hows. We have to accept, at this point, what Ajax seems to be saying, precisely as Tecmessa and the Chorus accept it.

A few moments later we receive our second surprise. The Messenger enters now with his story of perils ahead. Calchas has prophesied that this particular day is to be very dangerous for Ajax; for this one day alone he is to be exposed again to Athena's malice. If he survives this day he will have little more to fear, but it is obvious that for this one day it will be best for him to stay in seclusion. The Chorus summon Tecmessa that she may hear of this new development. When she takes in its import she utters one highly significant cry: 'I see that my lord has deceived me.' Then they all hurry out to find Ajax.

Before they find him we are ourselves transported to the place where he is, just in time to hear him begin his last speech. There is no suggestion that he had ever altered his

[1] Vv. 706-18, trans. Jebb.

purpose—not a sign that he even recalls what he has just said. As he proceeds it is evident that, far from having mellowed towards the Atreidae, he is even bitterer against them than ever; and, indeed, the whole host now is an object for his cursing. The relapse is utter and final, and there is nothing whatever to explain it. Of the reformed Ajax there is now no trace—as I say, nothing to suggest that he had ever existed.

How shall we grapple with this problem? To begin with, let us be clear about its nature. The problem is about a *drama*, not about some events that really occurred. If actualities were in question—if our problem were to fill some gaps in a sequence of historical fact—then explanations would be easy to come by: we could fetch them from far and near. We could accept (say) Mr Bowra's solution. He makes all hinge on Athena. Ajax did change his purpose, did reconcile himself with gods and men. Then he went out into the open—made the fatal mistake of leaving his tent—and this gave Athena her chance. Somewhere in the background we are to suppose that once more she was able to exert her influence on Ajax; once more she has him at her mercy. It is she who reverses his mood and makes him think, once again, of destroying himself. He imagines that he is acting freely, 'but he is really the victim of her curse'.[1]

I do not feel that this view can stand for a moment. We know that Athena is Ajax's enemy, and we know that it has been pronounced dangerous for him to go abroad on this day. That amounts to a general awareness; it by no means allows us to reach the specific conclusion that Athena was responsible for his act. Mr Bowra goes so far as to declare

[1] *Sophoclean Tragedy* (1944), p. 44.

that Ajax is no longer 'master of himself'—that he has, in effect, relapsed into madness—but this is a notion that we can test directly by the drama. Is there the slightest sign in that final speech that Ajax is not in complete control of his faculties? The truth is that Mr Bowra has wrested the play into this shape in order to secure a pattern that he feels should be in it, for if Ajax kills himself in madness it is clear that he cannot be blamed for doing so, and this is how it should be. Sophocles 'would not send this great being to his death in an unchastened, unrepentant spirit'.[1] As the Ajax who seems to die so obdurately is merely an Ajax out of his mind, the last *true* Ajax we glimpsed was the Ajax of that humble, reverential speech. We may reply that it is merely a question of fact. Ajax in his last speech is unchastened, and, if words have any meaning, Ajax in that last speech is sane. The trouble with Mr Bowra's theory is that it quite ignores the natural impressions. It is eminently the kind of theory that one reaches in one's study when one ponders and broods and deduces.[2]

There are really two questions that we have to answer.

---

[1] *Op. cit.*, p. 40.

[2] The principle involved here is really of the utmost importance and could be set out more fully as follows:

Dramatists are sensible people. They write, therefore, to be understood. They know that theirs is a difficult art, and that many subtleties may not at first register. But they know that if a *main meaning* fails to register they will have done their work to no purpose. Dramatists therefore take pains that their main meanings shall be immediately clear: they do not seam their plays with main meanings that have to be extracted from the drama by force.

It follows that if a critic presents us with a main meaning that he has extracted from the drama by force, a strong presumption exists that this meaning was never really present in the drama.

(1) What was Ajax supposed to be thinking when he uttered that monologue of resignation? Did he really mean what he said, or was the greater part of it an elaborate pretence? (2) What was the point of it all? What dramatic strategy was Sophocles pursuing?

I do not think that the first question (though complex) is difficult; it is the second question that is hard.

On the first question I will put down what seem to me to be the decisive items, in the order of what seems to me to be their importance.

(1) First and foremost there is that cry of Tecmessa's after she has learnt of the prophecy of Calchas: 'Well see I now that I have been outwitted by my lord.' In effect she says: 'How blind I was! Of course, he meant to do it all along—he never changed his mind for a moment.' The truth flashes on her as soon as she hears that the day is unlucky; it is immediately obvious to her that *that* is the underlying sense of the warning. A moment later she cries: 'O come, be quick! no time for lingering if we would save a man who seeks to die.' Her thoughts do not envisage external danger: she knows instinctively what she has to expect. We cannot possibly say that Tecmessa is wrong, cannot possibly pit our judgment against hers, for that would be to deny the very nature of drama. We could question what she says only if we knew more of what had been going on than she does, and that is simply not the case. It will often turn out, in a problem like this, that there is some insignificant-seeming detail that is crucial; I suggest strongly that this lament of Tecmessa's is crucial. Let us put ourselves in Sophocles' place. If he had meant that first speech of Ajax for genuine, could he conceivably have made Tecmessa utter this cry?

That would have added sheer pointless confusion—would have brought the drama to the verge of chaos.

(2) I think that the clue next in importance is the abruptness with which the second speech begins—or the smoothness, if we look at it that way, with which it resumes a mood never broken, an intention never for one moment abandoned. If a change of mind had really occurred, then an explanation of some kind would have been essential, and it is difficult to believe that Sophocles would have withheld it. It is not as if there were technical difficulties. There were no real difficulties at all. Six words at the outset of the speech would have sufficed to put us on the track.

(3) There are, finally, those vaguely bodeful lines with which the earlier speech concludes. I would insist again that they could not *in their place* have constituted an effective clue. The tenor of the speech is too strong. We have no reason whatever, at this point, for assuming that Ajax has suddenly turned into a liar. He makes those flat declarations of changed purpose, and we are simply driven to accept them. But the final lines do gain significance in retrospect. From the vantage point of our later knowledge we seem to see what they really were: the last will and testament of Ajax. All this is after the event. But is it possible to believe that Sophocles would have written them if he had meant those earlier declarations for genuine?

What, then, was Sophocles driving at? What was the point of it all? Some German scholars (for example, Weinstock and Reinhardt) have felt that the deepest thoughts in the play are being presented to us in that first speech of Ajax: that, whatever may be the difficulties of interpretation, there is more in it than a mere will to deceive. This is a view that

I suppose we should all like to share. We seem to see the very deeps of Ajax. The critics I have mentioned work it out somewhat as follows. Ajax has received a genuine revelation. He sees his starkly individual attitude as untenable. He too must bow to the law of the universe, must take his part in the general system of being. But he sees it, so to say, in theory only, for he cannot change the essential Ajax. The Ajax reflected in this speech is the Ajax-who-might-have-been. His situation in this way is truly tragic; he has penetrated his illusions at last, but only when it is too late to act. Reinhardt considers that Deianira undergoes a somewhat similar crisis. She, too, utters a deceiving speech (436) but there is much more in it than deception, for she, too, is engaged—at least partly—in clarifying the truth to herself. She and Ajax see themselves as part of the All—see also where right conduct would lead them. For Deianira it would have meant quiet submission, for Ajax a reconcilement with his enemies. But though their eyes are open to the truth they cannot make it *wahr* and *wirksam* for themselves.

This is an interesting view, yet one is justified in doubting, I think, whether we are much advanced by it in our grapplings with this matter. We take off into rarefied metaphysical air. But there is a hard central core to this problem. There are those unequivocal assertions of Ajax: he is going to bury his sword, he is going to make peace with the Atreidae. We are always brought back to these.

It is extremely difficult, no matter how one looks at this question, to feel that Sophocles' prime interest was in mental fluctuations as such. Even if we interpret the first speech as meaning that Ajax really did change his mind, we must still ask: what is the upshot? A lightning change in one direction, following by a lightning change in another, and no clarification of motive, no clear hint to us of the cause of it all: this would have been sheer waste of dramatic time. For the very function of drama is to reveal. Drama does not exist to perplex and to hide, but to give us insight into the meaning of behaviour; and it is to be emphasized that in this case we need the dramatist's help, are simply not in a position to work the matter out for ourselves. The case of Deianira is interestingly different. She, too, seems to change without warning and with no explanation offered. She has determined, she says, to take no action against Iole, but to reconcile herself to the new situation. Then she goes into the house. When she comes out again after the *stasimon* it is to tell us of the action she is taking: she is going to try the effect of the love charm on the robe she is about to send to Heracles. Here, at first sight, is a parallel to the sequence we are studying in the *Ajax*. Mr Webster even finds it decisive. But the parallel is not really genuine. The change in Deianira may be a surprise, but it is hardly a problem, for it is precisely the way we might have expected her to act in the first place. It was her meekness that a little astonished us; when she decided to revert to her woman's nature we are not hard put to it to comprehend the why and the wherefore. But with Ajax we *do* need illumination, and Sophocles gives us no light at all.

The psychology, then, we take it, is pointless; nothing transpires from the seeming changes in Ajax; we are plunged into bafflement and left there.

Let us assume, however, that Sophocles was not concerned with psychology, that his preoccupation was with plot.

It is clear that the materials were at hand, hereabouts, for a very arresting dramatic sequence—a sequence with a number of shocks in it. We begin with those apprehensions about Ajax: his friends are expecting the worst. Then there is the sudden relief: they all draw their breaths again. Then the Messenger arrives with his news and once more there is dire foreboding; and this time the worst occurs. It is a familiar pattern in fiction. Now let us think what the handling of it meant. The Messenger will, of course, arrive too late and his news will have the effect of a bombshell. It is clear that it can have this effect only if it falls into tranquil minds. This is to say that Ajax must have fully satisfied his listeners that he was meaning no harm to himself. Here was the heart of the problem, for Ajax's friends are not easy to satisfy. They are by now very much on the alert—a thin pretext would not have sufficed. Sophocles then (if he wishes all the shocks in his sequence to have value) has the task of devising a speech that will sound very sincere indeed. He did this—did it perhaps only too well. The speech, at any rate, quite hoodwinks Tecmessa and the sailors. But now this further consequence follows, that Sophocles has hoodwinked his audience as well! For I suggest that this really happened. The audience have no advantage over the friends of Ajax in knowledge. They enjoy no 'inside' information, and it is not really practicable to supply them with any. The only thing that Sophocles can do is to try to introduce into the speech some overtones that may (possibly) reach the ears of the audience, while they miss those of Tecmessa and the sailors. It may be that that is what we see him attempting in those last ten lines of the speech. But even that attempt failed. (The proof is that we are still debating the matter.)

Sophocles could not resolve this problem; it was a veritable technical *impasse*.

I add one additional note. Whatever the conclusions we reach they should be based on experience that is *possible*. Jebb, for example, took the view that 'while the change of purpose is feigned, the change of mood is real'.[1] It seems to me quite out of the question that those two things can be grasped together; if a reader grasps the one he certainly will not grasp the other. Again, there is the question of irony. Mr Webster is one of those who believe that Ajax really did alter his purpose, yet the audience, he thinks, will feel irony, because they know that, despite this change, Ajax will take his life sooner or later. I think that this misconceives the reaction. The feeling of irony arises when two sharp awarenesses clash; one must be in control of one's facts, so that one can relish their piquancy in an instant. As the Athenian audience listened to this speech their dominant feeling, I am sure, was astonishment, and I doubt whether this would have left room for much else, save for a few rapid and half-formed speculations about the next probable turn of the plot.

For a last point: analogies need watching. Pohlenz brings forward as parallels the disguised Odysseus talking to Penelope and Agamemnon 'proving' the host. But these are not parallels at all, for in these cases we are in a position of vantage: we can see all round what is happening. In the *Ajax* we enjoy no such privilege: we are on a level with Tecmessa and the sailors. That, indeed, was the essential difficulty, the trap in which Sophocles was caught.

[1] *Op. cit.*, p. xxxviii.

CHAPTER VI

SOPHOCLEAN MELODRAMA:
THE *TRACHINIAE*

ONE of the chief snares in criticism is the natural impulse to pick out from any given work what is interesting—to trace in it what seems the significant pattern and to shut one's eyes to the rest. In the case of an ancient work, especially, this can often result in a most attractive and persuasive appraisal; indeed, to go from the appraisal to the original work may be a disappointing experience. The clean lines of the interpretation may seem blurred, the sharpness of the import dulled. Yet the task of criticism is to be faithful: not to remake the work, but to recover it; not to select from it a pattern that engages, but to take and retain the whole impress.

Of all the dramas of Sophocles perhaps the *Trachiniae* tempts most to this critical making-over. It is perhaps the oddest play of Sophocles that we have: not so odd in construction as the *Ajax* (for this time the *reason* for the construction is clear) but odder in its assemblage of parts. More accurately, it is the mixing of strains that is curious. There will be a patch of what seems like primitive saga, then a scene of painstaking and meticulous realism. The events seem to come from different systems—to belong to different levels of reality—and even the human beings, as critics have remarked, fail to match. Heracles and Deianira do not meet, but in any case it would be very difficult to imagine them together: their *genera* seem so incongruous. And, indeed, there is very little that is common between the two Deianiras themselves: the Deianira who was wooed by the river-god, and the fully-realized woman whom we see and hear in the play.

The elements are strangely assorted. There is a rich array of human feelings and motives; intermixed with these there are marvels and miracles; and there is a good deal that is in between—personality that is not quite human, motives whose sources seem mysterious and beyond our conjecture. The essential problem is to assess the result. Add the elements together, and what kind of a play have they made?

Dr Gilbert Murray has given us one answer—a very clear and definite answer. For Dr Murray the pattern of the drama is plain. The drama is about the relationship of a man and woman, and the man and the woman are representative types. 'Some of the great tragedies of the world are built, like *Hamlet* or the *Oresteia* or *Oedipus*, on some strange and rare combination of incidents; some, like the *Medea*, the *Alcestis*, perhaps the *Bacchae*, are seen happening all about us in every age.' Dr Murray thinks that the *Trachiniae* is of the latter kind. 'You can see Heracles and Deianira most Monday mornings in some police court or other, as you can see in Broadmoor asylum Medeas who have murdered their children.'[1] This is persuasively put. Dr Murray means that Deianira is the eternal type of the loving wife who is wronged, Heracles the type of her ruffianly master. For Dr Murray Heracles is unmitigated brute—Bill Sikes raised

[1] *Greek Studies* (1946), p. 126.

to the status of hero—a vulgar, coarse, insensitive, loud-mouthed villain. Indeed, Dr Murray feels that this was the underlying motive of the play: to strip from the hero his spurious splendour. Dr Murray imagines Sophocles as engaged in 'defacing or restamping the coinage', as setting out to obliterate the false legend of Heracles and to affix on him the right label for ever.[1]

I cannot help feeling that this is a very much simplified picture and that what Dr Murray is really doing here is giving way to the enticement of abstraction. He is not truly describing the play; he is describing what *interests* him in the play. He is selecting from its whole pattern one of its patterns, and is offering this to us in place of the whole; and I think that he even distorts this pattern in order that it may come out more clearly to his liking.

Let us study the case more fully. We may begin with the question of Heracles. It must be confessed that the general impression of him is not very attractive. Our first report of his doings comes from Lichas. More than a year before this he had gone to stay with Eurytus, had had continual disagreements with his host, and on one occasion had been thrown out of the house for drunkenness. Watching his chance to get even, he had treacherously murdered Eurytus' son, catching him in an absentminded moment and hurling him down from one of the heights of Tiryns. For this he was punished by Zeus and sent for a while into servitude; after which he got even once more by killing Eurytus and sacking his city. This is the first version of these events that we are given; but after a little the first account is revised. It seems that Heracles sacked Oechalia not out of vengeance,

[1] *Op. cit.*, p. 106.

but as his ruthless way of obtaining a girl that he wanted; and this girl, Iole, he now coolly sends home, expecting Deianira to see to her lodging. It has not even occurred to him to feel qualms about the matter: he has taken Deianira's acceptance for granted. It is true that there is no great novelty in the arrangement: we learn from Deianira that Iole is but the last of a series. Even so there is a certain difference: Deianira is older now, while Iole is in the bloom of youth and is clearly a particular favourite.

Then his fate catches up with Heracles. As the poison begins to take effect his behaviour runs true to form. He bellows for his herald Lichas and, when he has learnt for a second time that the robe came from his wife and no other, takes the innocent Lichas by the ankle joint and dashes his brains out against a rock. Then he indulges in awe-inspiring antics, flinging himself on earth or leaping into air, and screaming so that the headlands ring, while the people stand in a cowed circle and watch. At length he bids Hyllus lay him on a bier and have him carried home to Trachis. He arrives breathing threatenings and slaughter against Deianira. When, at long last, he is induced to take in the fact that Deianira is dead—self-slain for her terrible mistake—he gives no sign of emotion. His mind is already running ahead on oracles, and what this news may signify for his own destiny. Then he delivers his final commands. Hyllus is to light his pyre (at the very least, to prepare it) and to take his concubine Iole to wife. Hyllus' feelings revolt, but he is obliged in the end to submit.

It is not an attractive picture, and at first sight it might well seem that Dr Murray's view was the true one, and that the root notion of Sophocles here was to lay the legend of

Heracles in ruins. Certainly the case against the hero looks black. He would seem, on a summary estimate at least, to deserve every name Dr Murray calls him—and perhaps a few others as well. And yet if we look a little more closely at the drama I think we shall see that this view, after all, cannot hold.

Consider this sentence of Dr Murray's: 'Sophocles has taken the same heroic figure [as Euripides took in his *Heracles*], accepted by certain traditional standards as "the best of men" but has emphasized the utter savagery and brutality of those standards, and—most surprising of all—has shown us the whole miserable story through the eyes of one woman, and presumably the one who suffered most.'[1] 'Through the eyes of one woman'—that is true: the story, or a very considerable part of the story, is seen from Deianira's point of view. But what is this point of view? Deianira adores her husband. 'To her joy', she tells us in the prologue, he came to save her from Acheloüs, the river-god; in his long absences she yearns for him continually; she is full of anxiety for his safety; she rates her life a thing of no worth until his return. All this cannot but affect us, and the dramatist means it to affect us. Heracles is established for us as a man of men, a man who, whatever his failings, has qualities that can command infinite devotion from a woman. And it is not only from Deianira that he can command it: the Chorus are at one with their mistress, Hyllus feels exactly the same. To the Chorus he is a hero 'most glorious'; even when he is brought low they still say, 'What a man!' When they see him in his agony they exclaim: 'Ah, wretched Greece, what mourning will be thine if this man is lost to

[1] *Op. cit.*, p. 113.

84

thee!' Hyllus accuses his mother, in his bitterness, of having slain the best man of all the world, whose like they shall not see again. This is the constant theme, that Heracles is worth the tears and the anxiety and the yearning, and we must accept it as seriously meant. We can test Dr Murray's thesis in this way: if Sophocles was really meaning to turn the legend seamy side out, then he must have been privately sarcastic every time he wrote 'best of men'. I do not think there is any escape from this. Dr Murray says that Sophocles gets his results not so much by intellect as by feeling. 'Euripides' thought is conscious and explicit; it often takes the form of argument. Sophocles' feeling is subconscious and overflows.'[1] We shall all admit a certain justice in this contrast. Nevertheless, it is a highly dangerous procedure to lay much responsibility on what is subconscious in a writer. It is obvious, from a glance at his plays, that the intellect of Sophocles is not usually in abeyance as he writes. The essential difference between Sophocles and Euripides is not that one of them feels and the other thinks, but that Sophocles thinks and feels always (or nearly always) as a dramatist, while there are times when Euripides seems to be wishing he were an essayist. In this case there seems to me to be no reason whatever for supposing that Sophocles was not well aware of what he was doing. If the play really does discredit Heracles, then Sophocles must have known that it did. But is such a thesis really possible? When the audience heard the words 'the best of men' can one doubt that they accepted them simply, without a suspicion of an undertone of satire? Heracles most certainly has his faults—some of them become glaring in the play. But he is still 'best of men'

[1] *Op. cit.*, p. 122.

in theory, and in many points of reality as well; and Sophocles does not seriously resist the idea.

The truth is that the virtues of Heracles still form part of the theme of this drama. We have caught the hero in some unfortunate moments, but we are not allowed to forget what he is and what he has been. He is still thought of as the deliverer from pests, as the liberator, the tamer, the toiler. He himself feels the irony of his plight, that he who has helped so many should now be so helpless himself.

Nor should we exaggerate even the unfortunate moments. Consider, for instance, the case of the captive women. Heracles has been gone for fifteen months. A messenger brings news that he is safe and that he has won a great victory. 'The household breaks into a paean of triumph, in the middle of which the herald, Lichas, arrives, leading a procession of broken-hearted women. Heracles has sacked the city of Eurytus and brought these captives. "These . . .", says Deianira, "in God's name who are they? They are pitiful!" And there they stand, in all their misery, before our eyes, while Lichas tells his story.'[1] The moment, so recounted, is affecting, but Dr Murray has made it a little more affecting than it is. What is the exact impression of this scene in the drama? Lichas enters, followed by the captive maidens. For the first few moments hardly anyone troubles to look at them—they are not important enough for notice. Deianira's one thought, naturally, is of her husband: the vital question is, is he alive? There are several more questions and answers before we come to the subject of the captives. Deianira then asks who they are. She is sorry for them, of course; she is a kindly woman, and all pitiable

[1] Gilbert Murray, *op. cit.*, p. 117.

people have her sympathy. But she is not emotionally upset about them, and she most certainly does not dream for a moment of being affected in her opinion of Heracles. The talk flows around and beyond them. Then, having satisfied her curiosity on other counts, Deianira turns to the maidens once more. She feels the pity of their state: how if one of them had been her own daughter! She is provoked to sad reflections: she is beholding one of those strange, harsh reversals of fortune that life brings and that one has to accept. Then we learn from her words one more thing—something that Dr Murray does not include in his summary; what we learn is that most of these captives are already steeled to their lot; indeed we gather that they are surprisingly cheerful. That is why Iole stands out—why she has caught Deianira's attention. Iole is the only one who is acting her part with propriety, the only one who really looks like a captive. All this is important for Sophocles' meaning. It is true that he has set these captives before us and given us the chance of dwelling on them, if we wish to, through the course of a scene. But he does not seem to be trying to lacerate our feelings. Dr Murray asks: 'Is Sophocles emphasizing the horror of it, or merely accepting it as natural?'[1] Sophocles does not quite accept it as natural, but on the other hand most certainly is not emphasizing the horror. He knows as well as we do that the enslavement of maidens is bad, but he does not *make a point* in this scene of their misery. He is not attempting, through them, to make us see Heracles as a monster.

And I think that much the same thing applies to some later episodes in the drama, where Heracles has incurred

[1] *Op. cit.*, p. 117.

general censure for offences of omission or commission. There is, for example, that callous reception of the news of Deianira's death. This, by almost general consent, shows an incredible coarseness of grain. Not to be touched at such a moment as that, not to show even interest in the news! Yet I think that one can misstate the matter. It is a question again, of the whole impression, and of the context in which this incident occurs. Hyllus is not aware of the full import of his words: he thinks that he is informing his father of one thing, while really he is informing him of two. The mention of Nessus the centaur blots out all else—even wives—for Heracles. It is not exactly that he is too sorry now for himself to spare a thought for any other person. No doubt he is sorry for himself, but self-pity is not his central emotion. It is rather that he is swept up into quite a different region of feeling. Everything has become suddenly plain: he sees the pattern of his life clear through to the end; and from now on his preoccupation is (so to say) to play out his divinely appointed role. There is no blasphemy in comparing the last phase of this drama with the last phase of the *Oedipus Coloneus*, for Heracles, too, has his part assigned, he too is semi-sacred from now on. It is not true, I think, to the atmosphere of this part to describe his injunction about the pyre as monstrous, for Heracles is speaking now with authority; behind his words are the grove of the Selli and his father's oak of many tongues. He *knows* what is right to do. That is why he bids his son be a man and brace himself for the repugnant task. His own end is impressive and solemn.

But what of the other command? Iole is forced on Hyllus. Heracles is quite insistent about this: Hyllus must swear that he will take the girl. Interpretation is harder here. The chief question, I think, is not of Heracles' motive in commanding this thing, but rather of Sophocles' motive in raising the issue at all. It would be strange if at such a late point in the play Sophocles were thinking of his hero's psychology, for we have passed beyond interests of that kind: the play has taken a larger sweep. Why return, at so solemn a moment, to make a last point about Heracles' temperament? And it is not as if we can have any confidence that we know what the point really is. Critics are about equally divided: some think we are seeing Heracles at his worst, some think we are seeing him at his best.[1] Perhaps what we have is egoism incarnate (he is resolved at all costs to keep Iole in the family); perhaps what he is meant to be revealing is a genuine concern for the girl. There is really no way of knowing from the drama; all we do, when we propound a solution, is invest the drama with what we consider, on general principles, to be likely. Jebb said that the passage was needed, 'if the poet was to avoid a contradiction which must otherwise have perplexed the spectators',[2] that is, it was one of those last-minute adjustments, of a kind so familiar in Euripides, that serve to square a drama with legend. It is not the sort of explanation one likes, but one is hard put to it here to find a better. If Jebb is right, then Sophocles makes the adjustment in his own un-Euripidean way: which renders it the more deceptive, for we incline to suspect in the exchange some significance that is not really there. We can only say that if there is significance for character, we do not know what it is. But I

---

[1] For example: 'It is not tenderness towards Iole, but a tribute to himself' (H. D. F. Kitto, *op. cit.*, p. 294); '. . . an unsuspected trait of tenderness and justice in Heracles' (C. M. Bowra, *op. cit.*, p. 142).

[2] *Sophocles: The Trachiniae* (1892), p. 176.

think we can take it for granted that in these last solemn moments of the drama Sophocles would not have thought of his hero as doing wrong. Heracles' acts are now really out of our sphere; he has now his own right and wrong; he is no longer answerable to ordinary laws. Perhaps Sophocles meant us to take the command as possessing (like the other) a mysterious authority that it was not for us closely to question.[1]

Let us turn now to Deianira. Dr Murray has not a great deal to say of her, but all that he does say is to her credit. Other commentators have been rather more critical. There are, to begin with, one or two problems not very different in kind from the two that we have just been discussing. Heracles has been gone fifteen months and Deianira knows that within this period his fate, one way or another, will be settled. She knows it from what he himself told her. Before he set out on this last journey he took her more into his confidence than usual—said things that seemed to mark the moment as serious; and he left with her an ancient tablet inscribed with characters foretelling his destiny: never before had he explained this writing. Besides all this he has taken the trouble to set his affairs in order; he has assigned to his wife her portion and set apart certain lands for his children. Obviously he feels the time immediately ahead to be critical, and he has made this very clear to his wife. Deianira has full reason to believe that if Heracles does not return by the end of this period he will probably not return at all. Yet she has been capable of an extraordinary passivity. Though the time

[1] It is interesting to speculate on the anthropological bases of the matter. Blumenthal (*Sophokles* [1936], p. 196) points out the odd suggestion of suttee: 'Perhaps once Iole *did* follow the hero on to the funeral pyre.'

has gone on, she has sent no messengers, she has made no inquiries, she has not even thought of confiding her anxieties to her son. The play opens at zero hour: the very time of fulfilment has arrived. Yet even now she has no idea where Heracles is, and still appears to have no thought of finding out. What does all this signify—reserve, timidity, dependence? Is there some strange inhibiting trait in her nature that makes it so difficult for her to take action? Is it natural for her to hide herself away from facts until, all of a sudden, the facts come crowding round her? What, in short, are we to deduce from her conduct? Or are we meant to deduce anything at all?

It is a neat little problem for interpretation, and I would suggest that the principle underlying it is simple. A drama is a work of art involving many delicate and difficult manipulations. Theoretically, everything that happens in a drama should form part of a tight-spun network; everything done or said by a character should have its proper, assignable reasons. On the other hand, the pressure of plot may sometimes put the dramatist in a difficulty. He may need a thing to be done or said—may need it very much for the sake of his action—and yet it may be very hard to make this thing seem natural. In the end, the problem may defeat him. What results then is quite a common thing in drama and may be described as a sort of transparency. We catch the dramatist, so to speak, at his game; his art, for these few moments, is not concealed; we look through what he is doing and see what he is about and why. As I say, these patches of transparency are found quite often in dramas, and are really of no great importance if we take them naturally for what they are. Audiences grasp their quality more easily than readers—very much more easily than sophisticated readers. They understand instinctively what is happening. They will be aware of a thinness in the drama—of something to be glided over—and will adjust their responses accordingly.

There is a classical instance in the *Oedipus Tyrannus*, not far from the beginning of the play. (It is, of course, near the beginnings of plays that these transparencies are most likely to occur: to get a play started smoothly is not always the simplest of matters.) When the *Oedipus Tyrannus* opens Oedipus has been King of Thebes for some time. But when his predecessor Laius is mentioned, this is the little exchange that occurs:

Creon. Laius, king, was lord of our land before thou wast pilot of this State.

Oedipus. I know it well—by hearsay, for I saw him never.

Creon. He was slain; and the god now bids us plainly to wreak vengeance on his murderers—whosoever they be.

Oedipus. And where are they upon the earth? Where shall the dim track of this old crime be found?

Creon. In this land, said the god. What is sought for can be caught; only that which is not watched escapes.

Oedipus. And was it in the house, or in the field, or on strange soil that Laius met this bloody end?

Creon. 'Twas on a visit to Delphi, as he said, that he had left our land; and he came home no more, after he had once set forth.

Oedipus. And was there none to tell? Was there no comrade of his journey who saw the deed, from whom tidings might have been gained, and used?

Creon. All perished, save one who fled in fear, and could tell for certain but one thing of all that he saw.[1]

Question and answer continue in the same strain.

Now, what are we to say about the vagueness of Oedipus

[1] Vv. 103-19, trans. Jebb.

here? He is not altogether surprised to hear that Laius was murdered: he admits to having heard some rumours of that. But it has never occurred to him to ask any questions; apparently he has had no desire to inform himself in detail of the facts. He has been, indeed, quite incredibly incurious. If we may judge from his tone in this passage he has been content to remain utterly in the dark about the place and the time and all the circumstances of the murder.

It is interesting to observe how some scholars approach this little problem. Consider, for example, Mr Sheppard's[1] comments. Creon tells Oedipus that Laius was the former ruler of Thebes. 'Oedipus need not be told this! Creon, realising the difficulty of finding the murderers, and also embarrassed at having to speak before the crowd, is slow in coming to the point.'[2] Oedipus says he knows by hearsay that Laius was king. 'Oedipus is now falling into the tone of a judge who examines carefully even the most obvious statement to see whether it is evidence. So, after a rather impatient, "I know that well", he corrects himself. Hearsay is not knowledge. The remark shows the character of the man.'[3] Mr Sheppard, that is to say, is uneasy. He feels the obvious incredibilities in the passage and he casts round for some way of smoothing them out. So he injects psychology into what is said. But surely such an attempt is vain. It is true that Creon begins somewhat hesitantly: he gives Oedipus a chance of hearing him in private. But does his feeling really extend to embarrassment, and can we possibly know that this is why he beats round the bush? As for Oedipus, Mr Sheppard's suggestions seem still more clearly

[1] Now Sir John Sheppard.
[2] *The Oedipus Tyrannus of Sophocles* (1920), p. 109.   [3] *Ibid.*

ideas that the critic is *supplying*, in order to give the passage a firmer coherence. But it is quite hopeless to try to give it coherence. Attempts to explain the difficulties by character in a sense do more harm than good, for they merely draw attention to the trouble; and of course the last thing that Sophocles wanted was that his difficulties just here should be noticed. I doubt if an audience would notice them: it would certainly not notice them seriously. It would notice them, if at all, with a shrug, seeing clearly what Sophocles was about. The one thing an audience would not do would be to assign the incredibilities to character.

We might sum up the matter in this way. The situation, when we look into it, is absurd. It is even a little more absurd than Aristotle admitted, for Aristotle argued that the element of the irrational here was at least something outside the action. But that is not really the case. The irrationality consists in the fact that Oedipus does not know how and where Laius died, and this ridiculous and incredible ignorance is something that occurs in the drama. It *is* ridiculous and incredible ignorance—if we allow it to affect us that way. Audiences know better than to do so; and, as for ourselves, our cue is merely to note the transparency and to trouble no further about it. The simple, self-evident explanation is that Sophocles did not quite conquer his problem. His problem was to make perfectly clear the essential data of the story. Strictly, he should have contrived to do this without violating natural likelihoods: should have engineered his exposition without giving away the fact that he was expounding. The task proved a little too awkward, with the consequence that we trip over the passage.[1]

[1] See also pp. 161 ff.

In the *Trachiniae*, I think, we have an exact parallel. The only difference that might be suggested is that the absurdity here is less glaring, which means that the temptation to interpret is stronger. I do not think that any of the interpretations can stand. Let us grant Deianira to be—what she obviously is—modest, self-effacing, self-doubting; even so, is it not asking rather much of us to believe that all this time she has done nothing? Surely at the end of the twelfth month—and still no word of Heracles' fortunes—she would have been driven in desperation to make some inquiry, or at the very least to talk over her anxieties with Hyllus. A woman, knowing that issues of life and death are in the balance and that a matter of weeks will decide them, does not, I think, allow reserve to carry her to such lengths of reticence as this. But, indeed, it is hardly necessary to argue the question, for one item, I would suggest, is decisive. Not only has Deianira said nothing to her son; Hyllus, equally, has said nothing to his mother. Prompted by the nurse, Deianira now mentions her worries to Hyllus, and it turns out that he is in possession of information about Heracles and, what is more, has been in possession of it for a considerable time.[1] Yet he has never passed it on to his mother. Here is a transparency if ever there was one, and surely it spreads to the whole situation. Sophocles is doing something very simple—getting his play off to as good a start as he can. It is by no means the smoothest of starts, but would it have been any smoother if at this juncture a messenger had arrived with up-to-date information about Heracles? Sophocles is asking us to concede him a little: his drama hereabouts will

---

[1] That, surely, is the natural impression—that he has been receiving progressive reports—not that he obtained all his news an instant before.

not bear to be *pressed* on. What he is striving for is an effect of crisis: of urgencies in the air, of destinies coming to a head. Many lines of fate are converging at this very point of time: the hour is even later than the eleventh, we are on the brink of the fateful minute. This was an effect worth getting and worth a little sacrifice of realism, and here we have the principal—indeed the only—reason for the strange passivity of Deianira and the odd taciturnity of Hyllus.

A second problem, though it has received more attention than the one just discussed, seems intrinsically of lesser importance. It is about Deianira and the *philtron*. Does Deianira decide to use it at once—immediately she has gleaned the full truth about Iole from Lichas—or does she form the plan somewhat later, when she has had leisure to meditate and brood? She and Lichas seem to reach an understanding: he on his part has told her the facts, she on her part seems to agree to accept the situation, and to make no overt move against Iole.

Lichas. Now, however, that thou knowest the whole story, for both your sakes—for his, and not less for thine own—bear with the woman, and be content that the words which thou hast spoken regarding her should bind thee still. For he, whose strength is victorious in all else, hath been utterly vanquished by his passion for this girl.

Deianira. Indeed, mine own thoughts move me to act thus. Trust me, I will not add a new affliction to my burdens by waging a fruitless fight against the gods.

But let us go into the house, that thou mayest receive my messages; and, since gifts should be meetly recompensed with gifts—that thou mayest take these also. It is not right that thou shouldest go back with empty hands, after coming with such a goodly train.[1]

[1] Vv. 484-96, trans. Jebb.

Has she a scheme already in her mind—that is, is she being insincere? Or does her mood alter when she is alone? Or is it perhaps half and half—has she some vague thoughts of what she may do?

The documentary ring of this question will be clear: indeed it is academic through and through. There is a principle of criticism that may sound trivial, but that has very great usefulness as a check and a guide: it is this: an audience has very little time to look backwards; it is too busy keeping up with events of the moment. (This is an inability that dramatists count on—one, indeed, that some dramatists abuse.) This question about Deianira would have no reality for an audience (just as it has no reality for a reader who reads currently). It is only when we *return* to the passage that we think of speculating about Deianira's intentions. If the play were a historical document, then we could allege that there were a few faint wisps of suggestion that might seem to point to a forming or half-formed design. Even then, we could have little certainty. When we look at the work as a drama the clues almost fade from sight.

Her change of purpose, when it comes, is not altogether (as I have said)[1] a shock. When she was pressing Lichas for details she was obviously *acting* a little. He is naturally anxious about the effect of his story—does not wish to be the one to break the news. She has to persuade him that she will not suffer unduly, that she can bear the very worst he may have to tell her. No doubt she felt she could bear it; now she finds that, after all, she cannot. The change of mood seems to me, as I say, on a different footing altogether from the violent fluctuations of Ajax, which are unaccountable in

[1] See p. 77.

97

themselves and which are left unexplained by the dramatist. Deianira's change is fully accountable. It is the most natural reversal possible—something that we are already more than a little prepared for.

A third problem is, I think, really important and leads us to the heart of the play. Is Deianira seriously at fault in making use of the philtre? Does her behaviour conform, in respect of this, to one of the conventional tragic patterns? Has she offended modesty, is she showing an upsurge of pride? What would Athenian audiences have thought of her—would they at this point have begun to frown?

Mr Bowra is quite sure that they would. 'By Greek standards Deianira is now open to severe condemnation'[1]; and he supports the view with historical instances. The duty of a Greek wife was to obey; it was understood that she might have to put up with an occasional concubine; in any case, magic was bad.

My own conviction is that historical instances serve no very useful purpose here, and indeed that their main effect is only to confuse. This is another way of saying that none of them is a real parallel, or comes close enough to the present situation to help. There is the question, for example, of 'hope'. 'The Greek notion of hope was not quite ours. It might sometimes do good, but it could also do harm. It was a mood of wild confidence, of unreasonable assurance'[2]; and Mr Bowra instances the unfortunate career of Croesus. Croesus most certainly hoped in a way that even a modern mind can see was foolish. But have those ridiculous hopes of Croesus any real relevance to Deianira's conduct? Herodotus gives a very vivid picture of Croesus: we understand

[1] *Op. cit.*, p. 127.   [2] *Ibid.*, p. 128.

his nature at once. He is the worst kind of incurable optimist, the most deplorable of wishful thinkers. He buoys himself up by signs, draws encouragement from the veriest trifles, is quite unable to control the future because the future to him is always in a rosy mist. Can such a nature shed much illumination on the case of Deianira? It is a datum of the *Trachiniae* that Deianira has reason to hope. We are in a sphere in which philtres are accredited—recognized as a part of reality—and there was no strong reason that she knew of why the word of the centaur should not have been trusted. She is facing a crisis in her life. If she wishes to preserve some semblance of happiness she must for once take the initiative strongly. A means of acting is at hand, and, as far as she can tell, the risks need not be counted excessive. Why is it 'a wild undertaking which defies modesty and sense'?[1] Even examples of dutiful wives must be used, it seems to me, with caution. Andromache says that she would be quite prepared to put up with a rival, for the sake of her dear lord Hector, just as in times past she accepted his bastard babes so as to cause him no vexation. But we must remember the context of this. Andromache is talking to Hermione and is giving her some timely advice. She is telling her that her strategy is bad—that a woman holds a husband by love and subtlety, and not by being jealous and exacting; and she drives home her point with this instance. Andromache no doubt was very loving by nature, but she was also a shrewd tactician: she understood the merits of flexibility and of the patient, indirect attack. Would Andromache, one wonders, have recoiled from the use of a philtre, if she had had one so temptingly ready to hand?

[1] *Op. cit.*, p. 129.

In short, there is this constant risk, in the historical approach, of coarsening the impressions of a play. Besides, why should we go outside the *Trachiniae* for help when we have the help of the Trachiniae themselves? We have expert advice on the spot. Greek Choruses are by no means invariably helpful, but surely we could not well expect to find sounder guidance just here than from these Trachinian women. They give us the standard feminine view. How much ought a woman to endure? When should she begin to fight for her rights? Which ways of fighting are fair ways? If we are not to trust the women of Trachis on such matters, whom, we may well wonder, are we to trust? And what they tell us is quite unequivocal. They think that the time has arrived when Deianira may well make a move; they do not think that she is rash or proud; and they even encourage her by reminding her that the only way to test the virtue of the philtre is to try it and see what happens. In short, nothing venture, nothing win, is their motto. Is it really possible to believe that when the Athenian audiences listened to these words their faces showed stern displeasure—that they muttered to themselves 'proud', 'immodest', and shook their heads in high discontent?

And this leads us to what is, I think, the crucial question about the whole play. If Deianira cannot in any deep sense be accounted responsible for the calamity that ensued, and if Heracles (for all his laxities and want of true husbandly devotion) can hardly be said to have brought his own hideous fate on his head, what type of play is it that Sophocles is offering, and what is the underlying meaning (if any) of it all?

It is generally understood that no drama is respectable

unless it shows character and circumstance interacting; every critic of Sophocles likes to think of the *Trachiniae* as respectable; so almost every critic exerts himself to prove that character and circumstance do interact. These efforts appear to me to be futile. Of course it would be very difficult to produce a drama that did not show some interaction of the sort, but before we call a drama a drama of character we should be sure that the influence of character is determining. A drama is not a drama of character merely because it requires certain broadly conceived types for its functioning. *King Lear* is a drama of character (it is many other things as well). But *King Lear* is a drama of character because the character of Lear is determining. *Romeo and Juliet* is not a drama of character, for the truly determining influences are elsewhere. It is obvious, of course, that a reasonable congruity must exist between a story and the people who figure in it. There would have been no tragic ending to *Romeo and Juliet* if Romeo had been a Henry V; and if Juliet had been unattractive, the story would not even have begun. A certain harmony, naturally, is assumed. But we need much more than this before we can talk of character as central. Deianira is beautifully drawn; we feel that we understand her; she is one of the most natural-seeming people in Sophocles. But she does not *produce* the events—there are other and far more powerful agencies at work. She does not do anything that is singular; many women would have acted as she did; in fact, it could almost be said that her action was typical of women. She was exceptional in possessing a philtre, not in her decision to try it. We can see what character really means in a play if we imagine Medea in her place; it is hard to fancy Medea contenting herself with a love-charm; character would then have taken charge indeed. But Deianira's act is not sharply individual; when we think of it we can apply it to many.

But again: we have no right, in discussing this play, to emphasize merely the strains that interest us, and, because we lack enthusiasm for marvels and magic, to discount their effect in this drama. To do this is to be genuinely unhistorical, for it amounts to projecting into the play a modern feeling. Whatever we think of marvels and magic, there they are—in the drama. They are more than a mere substratum: they are of the very stuff and substance of this play, and when we exclude them we are changing its nature. The disasters of this play do not really come from character; they come from the malice of a centaur, and because certain dooms have been foreordained: that is the kind of drama that Sophocles happens to be writing. The events are produced by magic unguents and come about in fulfilment of oracles. And the sensations, too, are important: the account of the shrivelling wool, the account of the physical agonies: these are not on the periphery of the play, they are very much of its essence. The *Trachiniae* has very much of its being in such pictures, and in sensational tableaux that match: a centaur slain in mid-river, a great clashing and bellowing of fighters, the writhings and shriekings of a hero in pain. It is a play also of pathetic humanity and of an oddly laboured, everyday realism (the Lichas-Messenger exchanges) that mixes strangely with what is so remote. But we do wrong to press for a point. No doubt every play should have its point, but the fact is that many plays lack one. What special point can Sophocles make: that women are often tender and patient, men often roving and crude? Is that a point of particular value? I would insist that no other point can be made: if we persuade ourselves we have found one it is merely because we have re-fashioned the play. The *Trachiniae* is a tragedy of a sort, but not a tragedy according to the rules. (Perhaps few Sophoclean tragedies are; perhaps no Sophoclean tragedy is.) If we call it high melodrama we shall not be indicating its fineness and truth, but there is no term that comes much closer to its quality, and at least we shall avoid the forcing on it of a tragic pattern that it does not possess.

CHAPTER VII

ROMANTIC TRAGEDY: THE *ANTIGONE*

WE may approach the *Antigone* through a short series of specific questions. In the first place, is Antigone herself in some way 'peculiar'? Is she a rather queer person—obsessed, psychologically twisted, abnormal? Some recent critics have found her to be so. Mr Edmund Wilson has no doubt of the matter. Mr Wilson had always felt Antigone to be strange. Then he read a discussion by Professor Walter Agard of those very debatable verses 904-20[1] and his suspicions at once crystallized into certainty: Antigone is unquestionably abnormal and (under Mr Agard's guidance) the hidden ways of her conduct can now be retraced.

Mr Agard, in brief, takes the view that nearly everything about Antigone is odd. There is the oddity of her hatred of Creon. She is opposing him, ostensibly, on a principle, but this is merely the superficies of their conflict: beneath it is the profoundest of personal antagonisms. Then there is the oddity of her relation with Haemon. It may be that she feels Haemon to be contaminated by Creon—finds the son repugnant on account of his father—but there seem to be deeper forces working than this. Is there an ambivalence in her attitude to marriage? On the one hand, it is her constant lament that by cruel fate she is to die a maiden; yet she never once refers to marriage with Haemon: 'such an outcome she

[1] *Classical Philology*, XXXII (1937), p. 263.

refuses even to consider'. Is there at the bottom of all this an 'emotional disturbance' caused by the horror of her parents' marriage? At any rate, though Haemon is her betrothed there is the strangeness of her utter want of attention to him. It would be impossible to ignore anyone more completely—Haemon does not seem to impinge on her life. She has not even a thought to cast in his direction, makes (unless verse 572 is hers) not one reference to him in the course of the play. Yet he appears to be an attractive youth, nor is there any positive suggestion that Antigone dislikes him. Finally, there is Antigone's own brother to be reckoned with: is Polyneices somehow at the heart of these problems? Mr Agard quotes Antigone's endearments: 'my own', 'my dearest brother', 'my own brother': and thinks that in these we have an unmistakable clue. They reveal a 'special intensity' of feeling. Antigone's is more than the natural love of sister for brother, and that is why she utters those crucial words in 909-12. She is disclosing what had always been true, that she *never* could have preferred a lover to a brother. She is giving her life for Polyneices, but, deep down, that is precisely what she wants. To be with Polyneices in Hades is, essentially, a 'more satisfying prospect' than to go on living with Haemon on earth.

Verses 909-12 are a problem in themselves and we may conveniently postpone them for the moment. I think that we may quite reasonably postpone them: long before they come we have formed our impression of Antigone, and it is the nature of this impression that is vital.

Let us begin with Antigone's feeling for Polyneices. Is there really an abnormal strain in her love? The endearments as such tell us nothing; in the circumstances they are not excessive. Is Sophocles resting perhaps, then, on a tradition—was it understood that Antigone had a special feeling for Polyneices? This supposition will not hold either. There was no tradition of that sort till much later.[1] Consider the treatment in the *Phoenissae* of Euripides. The relationship there between the two is perhaps closer, but it is still not abnormally close. The Antigone of the *teichoskopia* is an eager and excited girl, demanding (like Juliet at the ball) the name of each celebrity as he arrives. Naturally, she is on the watch for Polyneices; even so, he does not monopolize her interest; after she has identified him she continues with her excited inquiries. Nor is her behaviour in the sequel eccentric. The dead Polyneices is the brother who *needs* her; the dead Eteocles is not in danger of dishonour. And, after all, the general sympathies of this play have tended rather strongly towards Polyneices: his wrongs have been clearly shown, his side of the case has received very full statement. Eteocles, we are made to see, is a truculent and unscrupulous boor, who has never really intended to play fair. It would have been odd if the feelings of Antigone had been shown as drawn at all strongly towards him. But let us agree that Polyneices was her favourite. That is strongly suggested in the *Phoenissae*, less strongly, I think, in the *Antigone;* but let us concede that it was so. Need there be a profound significance in that? Grant a bond of especial affection between a brother and a sister, why should we rush into talk of fixations, and feel the love as in some way perverted?

The hate for Creon need not detain us; there is nothing in this that calls for discussion. They are deeply and unalterably

[1] Carl Robert points out that even in Statius no abnormality is suggested. (*Oidipus* [1915], vol. II, p. 122.)

at odds. No doubt in any circumstances there would have been little sympathy between them; the situation in the play merely brings to light every latent antagonism in their natures.

But the relation between Antigone and Haemon is curious, and raises principles of the highest importance. The nature of Mr Agard's approach will have been seen: he speculates about this matter precisely as if the case were thoroughly actual. How strange that Antigone should so ignore her betrothed! The play does not inform us of trouble between them, yet Haemon can give his life for Antigone, and still receive not the guerdon of a word. Is it then that 'she does not really care for him'? So Mr Agard proceeds to balance the alternatives, until fixation seems to offer the clue. As I have said, the one thing that invalidates such criticism is that it supposes a drama to be real. If the *Antigone* were a transcript of history—if it were in sober truth a slice of palpitating life somehow caught and put into print—then Mr Agard's speculations would have to be attended to and his solution itself might be sound. In the situation as it might actually have existed Antigone would have been bound to have some feeling for Haemon. Various possibilities can be imagined. Perhaps she loved him and fought down her feelings—because of Creon and all the new problems in her life; or perhaps she suffered some revulsion of feeling; or perhaps her love was deadened by pain and the dire part she was called on to play; or perhaps pride touched her a little and she could not bear that a son of Creon should help her; or perhaps she merely became, of a sudden, too busy, and there was no room in her mind for Haemon. In real life some such state of mind must have been hers, troublesome though it might be to identify it. Nothing is more important than to observe that no such 'musts' apply to the drama. It is often the very business of a dramatist to suppress—to take no cognizance of, actually to eliminate from his scheme —some quite large piece of the correspondent reality. The last thing that Sophocles wants here is a love-interest: that would have been a troubling irrelevance: any sign of it would have been a distraction. Haemon, of course, he requires: Haemon is the personal link between Antigone and Creon. Creon might have been punished in some general way for his sins, but only through a Haemon can the truth be brought home to him in personal anguish. Sophocles, therefore, needs Haemon; but then he immediately guards himself, so to speak, against paying the price of what he has bought. He *declares* the love between Antigone and Haemon, but *establishes* it only in the degree that is sufficient for his purpose. Haemon loves Antigone, we can see; but as for Antigone's feelings towards Haemon, they remain merely theoretic—exactly as Sophocles wished them to be. Her feelings towards Haemon are a blank—an empty space in the drama. There are vacuums of this kind in dramas—vacuums that in real life would have been filled, most certainly, by something; but in a drama they can remain unfilled. In short, we cannot answer the question, what Antigone's attitude to Haemon was. Critics give opposite answers, which is another proof that there is no way of knowing. The theory of the matter is that she loves him—that is absolutely all that the dramatist supplies, absolutely all that he wants us to think. To speculate further is merely to frustrate his intentions.

I would insist again on the principle. When we say, with Mr Agard, that Antigone 'never once refers to marriage with Haemon'[1] we are saying something that is perfectly correct. When we add the comment that 'such an outcome she refuses even to consider', we are saying something that falsifies the drama, for it raises an issue that Sophocles left quiescent, puts something *into* the drama that Sophocles (with every conscious care and intention) left out.[2]

I would suggest that we may dismiss all idea of Antigone as abnormal. She is, of course, a thoroughly exceptional person—that is why she gives her name to the play. But not a detail stamps her as 'queer' or neurotic; and, if we label her fixated, that is chiefly, I think, because we have a fancy for fixations as such and a desire, on principle, to find them.

What, next, of the act itself? Was Antigone right in doing as she did? In one sense the question is hardly worth asking. Her *view* of the matter is unquestionably the right one. We can resort to historical evidence if we wish, but in truth such evidence is almost superfluous; the evidence of the play is enough. We have our cue in the very first comment of the Chorus:

Such is thy pleasure, Creon, son of Menoeceus, touching this city's foe, and its friend; and thou hast power, I ween, to take what order thou wilt, both for the dead, and for all who live.[3]

This is notably reserved. When they hear that the edict has already been defied—that someone has given the corpse a mysterious symbolic burial—their thoughts fly at once to the possibility of divine intervention. Then we hear that there had been grumblings from the first, that certain of the citizenry had been restless under the edict. They went

---

[1] *Op. cit.*, p. 265.

[2] We can make far too much of Antigone's laments that she will never know the married state. They are in large part conventional for one in her situation. Compare Macaria.　　　　[3] Vv. 211-14, trans. Jebb.

wagging their heads in secret—malcontents who felt that no good could come of such an order. A second and a third time in the play we are told of this secret muttering. Antigone affirms that the discontent would be vocal, if only men's lips were not sealed by fear (504-5). Haemon roundly declares that the whole of Thebes is on Antigone's side. These references are quite decisive. Ismene, dismayed by the project, may exclaim against an act that 'defies the state' (79), but for us the phrase can have little significance: it only means that Ismene is overawed. In respect of power, Creon himself is the state; nevertheless, the moral feeling of the state is against him.

There is no question, then, as to theory: Antigone's view of the matter is the right one, Creon's view of it is the wrong. Creon has offended against a human decency, has violated a recognized fitness. But the query has still been put: even granting the rightness of her view, was it right for Antigone to act? Would not a wise passivity have been better? The issue, in a sense, was the gods' affair: should not Antigone, in Dr Gilbert Norwood's phrase, have been content to leave it to the gods to 'vindicate their own law'[1] if they wished. If she had done so, much less harm would have followed. The gods, no doubt, would have found a way—but a neater, tidier way. By Antigone's clumsy intervention the innocent suffer more severely than the guilty; it is a wasteful vengeance she unleashes.

I doubt if there is much real sense in this question. Even Dr Norwood, as he presses the point, finds the tragedy disappearing under his eyes. But the question, for one reason, is interesting: it is precisely the question that lies nearest the

[1] *Greek Tragedy* (1920), p. 140.

hearts of the Chorus; and the answer that the Chorus would have given would have matched Dr Norwood's exactly: Antigone was a well-meaning meddler, it would have been better for her not to have acted, she should have left the vindication of gods' laws to the gods. This would most certainly have been the opinion of the Chorus if we could have heard them reconsidering the action. It becomes of moment, then, to look at this Chorus—to examine, so to speak, its credentials—and the examination can have a typical value. It is true that there is no fully representative Sophoclean Chorus, but this Chorus is perhaps as representative as any. It departs in no marked way from the norm, it possesses no exceptional features. One imagines that among the lost plays there must have been Chorus on Chorus that resembled it closely. Let us study, then, this Chorus in some detail: following its moods as they vary and trying to estimate the value of its guidance.

The *parodos* is a song of gratitude for deliverance and of exultation in victory. It gives us the general setting, makes us feel the recent stresses and brings home to us the present relief. Then into this mood breaks Creon. The prohibition is clearly disturbing. The Chorus are not prepared to oppose it but they have no particle of enthusiasm for it. Creon himself is not quite confident of their attitude and gives them strong hints to be careful. He appoints them supervisors of the mandate—makes them responsible for seeing to its observance—and enjoins them not to traffic with those who might be likely to break it. They ask him if he imagines that they are seeking their deaths. At this point the guard enters with the news that the edict has already been broken. There is consternation, and, under dire penalties, the guard is dispatched immediately to find the offender and bring him to justice. As he goes, the Chorus launch into an ode.

Here we have one of the most famous odes of Greek tragedy, and it may seem ludicrously disrespectful to say of it that its function is to 'fill in', and yet that (in not too depreciatory a way) is its office. The guard has left on his quest for the culprit; in a few moments of dramatic time he will return with Antigone; there is an interval, therefore, to be managed. The obvious way is to charm the audience, which is what Sophocles proceeds to do. The two chief facts about the ode are these: in itself it is extremely beautiful, and its relevance to the play is nil. I do not think that the second fact can really be questioned. Mr Bowra has laid stress on the final verses, which seem to warn man against self-conceit: man is clever, but let him not think himself too clever: if he keeps the law, his city will stand, if not, he destroys its structure and will finish by ruining himself. 'It is not a hymn of praise to man's power, but something more complex and more closely related to the play'.[1] I do not think that this interpretation can possibly hold. 'Man's power' *is* the theme of three-quarters of the ode—that is a mere matter of statistics. As for the last quarter, which Mr Bowra picks out and asterisks, and in which he finds the heart of the whole, I would suggest that the natural impression it makes is not of a well-considered climax but of a rather hasty attempt at relevance before the song has quite run its course. The whole poem is tenuously 'occasioned' in the tidings that have just been brought in. What a wonder—and a curiosity—is man! How long is the tale of his

[1] *Op. cit.*, p. 84.

achievements, how marvellous the array of his talents! He has resource for everything—but Death. Then comes the final paradox of the poem, that man, though so cunning and skilled, will sometimes seem to court his own ruin:

Cunning beyond fancy's dream is the fertile skill which brings him, now to evil, now to good. When he honours the laws of the land, and that justice which he hath sworn by the gods to uphold, proudly stands his city: no city hath he who, for his rashness, dwells with sin. Never may he share my hearth, never think my thoughts, who doth these things![1]

I suppose there is a point here of a sort, but it can hardly be said to be a very sharp one. The thought (whether in the Greek or in the English) is rather muffled and hazy; and how are we to apply it to the matter in hand? This unknown person who has disobeyed the edict—is it of him that the Chorus are thinking? Do they regard his act as typifying anarchy as a menace to all civilized order? Yet this was the very offence that a few moments earlier they spoke of with awe—the very same act that they thought might be the work of a god. It seems obvious that there is no genuine connection. Their homily is so generalized and vague that it leaves the real issue untouched; and that, of course, was very much as Sophocles desired it. He is not anxious for a lucid comment just here. As for the Chorus as thinking beings—as a set of sentient, intellectual creatures—we must begin, from this point of the play onwards, to be careful not to take them too seriously: otherwise we shall soon be tearing our hair in distraction. Mr Bowra says of them that in their 'shock and amazement they try to relate what has happened to what is almost a philosophy of history, to explain their disapproval

[1] Vv. 365-75, trans. Jebb.

by general principles, and at the same time to justify these principles.'[1] But this seems to me to attribute to the Chorus a quite unbelievable cerebral intensity: their minds are not functioning at *that* rate. Indeed, it is difficult, from the evidence of the ode, to think of them as shocked and amazed at all. They have withdrawn into their own special realm, meditating gracefully at a distance; and this remoteness they preserve with great diligence through nearly the whole length of the action.

For it does become, from now on, a matter of real difficulty to shock them out of their ivory tower. They meet Antigone with a conventional reproach: already they are formalists, resolved to play safe. If we respond without prejudice to the action, we must already be feeling that there is little help to be looked for from the Chorus—little help, in a practical way, for Antigone; little help, in illumination, for us. There is a clear proof of that the very next moment. The guard makes his official report, and we have a little master-piece of subhumorous presentment. He is relieved to be done with the matter—is thoroughly glad to have saved his skin. But (though he makes a show of only wanting to be off) he cannot hide his disrelish; he is more than a little disgusted with himself, not at all proud of his part in this business:

Then we taxed her with her past and present doings; and she stood not on denial of aught—at once to my joy and to my pain. To have escaped from ills one's self is a great joy; but 'tis painful to bring friends to ill. Howbeit, all such things are of less account to me than mine own safety.[2]

Here a gust of true feeling comes in. This honest compunction of the guard is worth more to us even in guidance

[1] *Op. cit.*, p. 84.   [2] Vv. 434-40, trans. Jebb.

than the high-toned hortations of the Chorus. We—and the guard—are already ahead of the Chorus: have outstripped them in moral sensibility, see their attitude as inferior to ours.

The next *stasimon* is more naturally occasioned. Antigone is led away, guarded, and the Chorus begin their 'Blessed are they whose life has not tasted of pain'. Their thoughts turn to the ancient sorrows of the house (a minor, recurrent motif in the play) and they contrast with these human moils the changeless splendour of Zeus. Yet if we extract from this beautiful ode its quintessence of prosaic comment (a distressing process, perhaps, yet not without its instructive value) what we find is a meagre-minded conviction that Antigone was mad to do what she did. In the last verses there is an oracular dictum that may also be a side-glance at Creon: 'Wisely was that famous word spoken, evil will appear to a man to be good at the moment when a god lures him to destruction'; but the reference is heavily veiled: we could hardly catch its purport at the moment. In all that they put clearly into words the Chorus are the image of discretion. Creon, self-righteous and resentful, lectures the company vigorously on obedience. The Chorus have the appropriate reply: they say, quite simply, 'we agree'. When Haemon speaks in his turn, their comment is again, 'we agree': 'both sides have had something good to say'—a most perfect Chorus-like verdict. The ode on Love (781-800) is apposite enough but is hardly more than a lyrical interlude. It leads to the beautiful *commos* (806-82) in which Antigone laments her lot and the Chorus provide what comfort they can. In these lyric exchanges Antigone is somewhat stylized—retreats slightly from her personal reality to become an image of youth and goodness that suffers—yet her human lineaments are not quite lost. When she reassumes her personal voice the Chorus modify theirs to suit:

> Thou hast rushed forward to the utmost verge of daring; and against that throne where Justice sits on high thou hast fallen, my daughter, with a grievous fall. But in this ordeal thou art paying, haply, for thy father's sin.[1]

Their conclusion (again to extract the prose kernel) is that, though she acted, as she thought, for the best, yet it was madness to do what she did. Why contend against irresistible power? She has been guilty of a 'self-willed temper' and has, ultimately, only herself to blame.

Two choral odes remain, and only the first of these calls for comment. Antigone is taken away for imprisonment, whereupon the Chorus launch into their cavern song (944-87). It will be best to have this before us:

> Even thus endured Danaë in her beauty to change the light of day for brass-bound walls; and in that chamber, secret as the grave, she was held close prisoner; yet was she of a proud lineage, O my daughter, and charged with the keeping of the seed of Zeus, that fell in the golden rain.
>
> But dreadful is the mysterious power of fate; there is no deliverance from it by wealth or by war, by fenced city, or dark, sea-beaten ships.
>
> And bonds tamed the son of Dryas, swift to wrath, that king of the Edonians; so paid he for his frenzied taunts, when, by the will of Dionysus, he was pent in a rocky prison. There the fierce exuberance of his madness slowly passed away. That man learned to know the god, whom in his frenzy he had provoked with mockeries; for he had sought to quell the god-possessed women, and the Bacchanalian fire; and he angered the Muses that love the flute.

---

[1] Vv. 853-6, trans. Jebb.

And by the waters of the Dark Rocks, the waters of the two-fold sea, are the shores of Bosporus, and Thracian Salmydessus; where Ares, neighbour to the city, saw the accurst, blinding wound dealt to the two sons of Phineus by his fierce wife—the wound that brought darkness to those vengeance-craving orbs, smitten with her bloody hands, smitten with her shuttle for a dagger.

Pining in their misery, they bewailed their cruel doom, those sons of a mother hapless in her marriage; but she traced her descent from the ancient line of the Erechtheidae; and in far-distant caves she was nursed amid her father's storms, that child of Boreas, swift as a steed over the steep hills, a daughter of gods; yet upon her also the gray Fates bore hard, my daughter.[1]

Is there a deep design in this ode? Mr Bowra argues that there is. At first glance one would not, of course, think so. It appears to be lyrical embroidery of the reminiscent or associative sort. Antigone is to be immured in a cavern: well, a natural opportunity is given to recall other cases of the kind. Choric relevance can vary greatly: it is possible for it to be close and precise; but again it can be a loose formality. One would certainly have said, off-hand, that the relevance here was of the latter kind, and Mr Bowra's reasonings do not much disturb that impression. He considers that the three stories dealt with (of Danaë, Lycurgus and Cleopatra) are intended to have real significance, as suggesting to us three ways of looking at what is now happening to Antigone herself. He thinks that the final verdict is, so to speak, left open: any one of the three interpretations may be right. Danaë's imprisonment came about through a strange fate and redounded in the end to her benefit; perhaps it may be this way with Antigone. Lycurgus reviled a god and was

[1] Vv. 944-87, trans. Jebb.

made to pay the penalty for this; perhaps Antigone has been found arrogant, and perhaps she too is deservedly punished. The case of Cleopatra is 'more difficult to unravel'[1]; it is not altogether clear what legend is meant. But, at all events, Cleopatra was innocent: she did not deserve to be imprisoned. So here a third key is held out to us. The Chorus are suggesting that Antigone may be an innocent sufferer, that what we are witnessing is wanton brutality. Somewhat non-committally, they leave us to work out the matter for ourselves; but their song means, at least, that they have 'begun to waver': they have 'weakened', they 'temporize and cannot make up their minds'.

I do not think that Mr Bowra's view can possibly apply. It is invalid on a number of counts. His initial assumption is unwarranted: 'The mere parallel of imprisonment—and in Cleopatra's case it is uncertain and not mentioned—cannot explain all that the song means. It must have some more pertinent reference to the situation.'[2] One can only ask: why? The assumption that every ode must be relevant —must bear deeply and truly on the issues—is simply not borne out by the facts: Greek drama is packed with odes that do not possess this close relevance. Again, it is evident that even on Mr Bowra's reading the deeper import remains very confused. The Chorus do not really offer a clue, they distract the audience, rather, with a problem. On the first supposition, Antigone is innocent; on the second supposition, she is guilty; on the third supposition, she is innocent. What could an audience possibly have made of such guidance? Thirdly, there is Mr Bowra's image of the Chorus as an assemblage of feverish thinkers, passing through

---

[1] *Op. cit.*, p. 105.　　　　　　　　　　[2] *Ibid.*

emotional crises, racking their brains to get at the facts: as a set of thinkers who waver, who really struggle with their thoughts, who try desperately to make up their minds, who are seen as gradually working round to a decision: when every ode from this Chorus and almost every one of their utterances of whatever kind have stamped them in the clearest fashion as a company of poetic woolgatherers. But one word of Mr Bowra's is enough: he speaks of the difficulty of 'unravelling'. A word like unravel is the clearest symptom of something wrong in the critical process. No word could have less relevance to a drama: it is a word that one could only use when forgetful of what one is really discussing. I do not mention the inherent poverty in what Mr Bowra supposes the Chorus to be offering: was it in any case worth their while to labour such meagre suggestions? The essential thing is that such a method of approach does violence to the very nature of drama. No doubt whatever can exist that Sophocles the practising playwright (or Sophocles the writer of drama) would have seen such a venture as hopeless. The meaning that Mr Bowra extorts is a meaning that no drama could carry, so that once again the inference is immediate, that Sophocles never had a thought of conveying it.

It is shortly after this that the Chorus do something exceptional: for the first time in the drama they *act*. We may count as an act, perhaps, their definite assertion that they believe in Teiresias; and they take the unprecedented step of offering Creon some positive advice: they tell him to release the maiden and to make a tomb for the dead. Creon (startled) accepts their counsel without question. They break then into their Bacchus ode. No one could be insensitive to its soaring poetry or fail to perceive the extraordinary value of its placing. Its echoes are still in our ears when 'they are dead' (1173) drops like a plummet. The duties of the Chorus are now nearly over. They have little part from now on save in asking suitable questions and murmuring suitable agreements. They have a few pious maxims to utter and perform their office of concluding the play.

Is it not a melancholy record—if we think of them as real participants? How the function of a Sophoclean Chorus seems to dwindle when we scrutinize it closely like this. 'Sane and independent spectators', 'a fixed norm by which to measure the characters': these are the conventional generalizations. How much meaning is left in them when we really examine what a Chorus does? Is the Chorus of the *Antigone* an actor? On the contrary, as we have seen, not until the drama is nearing its end does this Chorus make a single move that even loosely could be interpreted as action. Is this Chorus an idealized spectator? Is it a personified reflection on the action, does it 'incorporate the sentiments of the poet'? We can only reply that we hope not, for we seem in general to do better for ourselves. And how often does this Chorus of the *Antigone* do what Schlegel thought he saw it as doing—give back to the spectator a finer expression of his own responses to the action? Does it do that even once in the play? The Theban Elders are far from being ideal spectators. They are wavery-minded, anxious-hearted spectators, who have private interests in what is proceeding. They have decided almost from the beginning to be neutral, to avert their eyes as far as possible from unpleasantness, to risk nothing but the safe abstraction. How much is this sanity worth? What is the value of this independence? The cynical, warm-hearted guard has more independence than they. Finally, do their odes reinforce the theme, restate it on another level, detach in a lyrical expression the very *Grundgedanken* of the drama? Hardly: the odes are for the most part tangential. The word is accurately used, for that is precisely what the odes do: they fly off at tangents from the theme. The truth of the matter, surely, is that the odes of the *Antigone*, with hardly an exception, are poetical arabesques: they charm, they relieve, they lull, they make pauses, they furnish transitions, they make effective 'curtains' and contrasts. Rarely or never in this drama do they give wings to an authentic dramatic emotion. As for guidance, we have no need of the services of this Chorus: we outgrow them in the first hundred lines.

To return to our original question: should Antigone have acted or not? Obviously the question has very little point. She did what she did because she was Antigone. It is not quite fair to judge her in retrospect, and in the light of all that followed. Her problem concerned herself and Creon: she could not have foretold the consequences. If the consequences had been spread before her, then the nature of her problem would have been different and we do not know how she would have acted. That, in any case, would have been another story. She faces her actual problem and is ennobled by the way in which she solves it.

Let us pass to the question of the structure. It would be too much to say of the story of Antigone that it is doomed to be either a prologue or an epilogue; that, certainly, would be too extreme a statement. But it would be perfectly truthful to say of it that it has a natural gravitation towards one or other of those roles.[1] In itself Antigone's story lacks staying power: there is hardly enough in it to make a full drama. Her deed done, her story is nearly over: there is not much more she can do but suffer the consequences of her audacity. We can see the effect of all this, structurally, in the *Antigone*. Indeed, the plan of this play offers a subtler study than either the *Trachiniae* or the *Ajax*. The *Antigone* is by no means patently of the diptych form; there is no sharp division, as in those other two dramas: the play does not fall into halves. Rather (as I have suggested)[2] what we have is an imperceptible glide from one main theme to another. It is Antigone who first arrests our interest, and at first the drama seems focused on her. Then she begins to lose ground in the drama; gradually she edges away until Creon is left occupying the centre. The final phases have their effectiveness, but the identity of the drama has changed. As I have said, it is not really an exaggeration to declare that in the last hundred lines or so Antigone is forgotten: she has by now become incidental to what has turned into a tragedy of Creon. This, I think, is the true curve of the drama, and it is not really possible to explain it away. It is emphasized by the entry of Eurydice. Between Antigone's deed and Eurydice's death no *nexus* whatever exists. Eurydice dies because Haemon dies: it is not necessary for her even to be aware of the prime cause of the whole fatal sequence. Her death, so to say, is just one consequence of the generalized folly of Creon. And we see the same curve in the underlying thought of the play. At first there was a very clear conflict between differing conceptions

---

[1] Compare the final phase (whether Aeschylean or not) of the *Septem*. It is possible that in the Euripidean *Antigone* the story of Antigone's deed was spoken by her as prologue. [2] See p. 52.

of law. On the one hand was a human edict, on the other a higher imperative. On the one hand was the force of the state, on the other an unspoken authority: we can formulate the clash in a number of ways; its essential nature is plain. But what happens to this dominant theme in the final phases of the play? It, too has receded into the background—indeed, has almost dropped out of sight. The play, in its later phases, is no longer about a conflict of law; it is about stubbornness and self-will, about the sin of refusing to listen, about a man who would never be told. All this is a far cry, again, from the opening motifs of the drama.

This change must just be accepted. In drawing attention to it we are not damning the drama, we are making a critical notation; and it is far better to admit what happens than to look for ways of retrieving the drama. Call it *Creon*, it is sometimes said, and every difficulty will be seen as unreal. This seems to me counsel of despair. Good acting can do much for Creon, but there are limits to what acting can do, and I doubt whether the best acting in the world could turn the *Antigone* into Creon's play. No: the *Antigone* is rightly named. The simple fact of the matter is that there is not enough of Creon to sustain a drama. Antigone is of tragic stature: Creon does not approach within hail of it. He is, in essence, an uninteresting man, commonplace in all but his obstinacy—that, it is true, is on a dangerous scale. But he talks more prosily than any other character in Sophocles. His maxims are consistently platitudinous, his lectures must have set off many yawns, judging by the specimens that we hear. As for his reasoning powers, they are puerile. That is what Haemon complains of. Haemon himself is mature, and feels the natural exasperation of the mature at exhibitions of mental ineptitude. Morally, it is the same: Creon's attitudes are those of a child. His chief reason, after all, for standing pat—a reason he as good as avows—is that he won't let any woman say she has beaten him. His repentance itself is uninteresting—one uses the word with a sense of unreality. There is no drama, no struggle, in the change. He receives a shock, that is all; his nerve goes, and, in a moment, he repents. There is something faintly blasphemous in suggesting that the play could be as well called by his name.

Creon's remorse, strictly speaking, is contrived—it is by no means dramatically established, the *processes* of it are non-existent—and that may lead to one further aspect of the structure. The *Antigone* for the first half of its length has the veritable tone of deep tragedy, but with Haemon's entrance a certain change becomes noticeable. Haemon's love (as we have seen) is a structural link: only through some such linkage could the punishment of Creon become personal—become dramatic, that is to say, and a fit subject for story. His retribution, accordingly, has a quality in it of accident. If Creon had not had a son Haemon, and if Haemon had not loved Antigone, he might conceivably have gone scot-free. The linkage is artificially forged. The play is not damned because of it, but it remains true that the structure is not of the tightest. Another sign is in what we have noted, that half the Antigone-Haemon relation is suppressed. On the one side—Antigone's—it has no dramatic existence, being quite irrelevant, in itself, to the dominant themes of the play, and to Antigone's own master passion of piety. It is very much of the nature of a postulate introduced by Sophocles for reasons of structure. But postulates in a drama have a slightly weakening effect. I think, also, that in other ways the tension relaxes somewhat. If we attend to the last speech of Antigone we shall become aware of a diversity of strains: there is much in it of romantic pathos: and that is the tone of the ode that follows. The final events are severe, yet removed a little by the fact of narration; and though Creon's own anguish racks him we realize (if we let our thoughts wander to Lear) how little of Creon there was, after all, to be racked. Creon is not permanently shattered—he lacks the capacity for that; his talent for suffering is not vast. It is in these ways that there is some relaxing. The *Antigone* is a wonderful drama, but we need not be overawed by an imaginary perfection. It opens in the tensest of veins, drawing its strength from conflict of character, and from the sheer arrestingness of one character. It departs somewhat from this promise. With the fading of Antigone the texture loosens and there is a slight change in the quality of the drama. We come perhaps as close to this quality as we can if we call it the quality of romantic tragedy.[1]

There remain one or two matters of detail: only one of them is, properly, a problem.

Everyone knows the experience of gazing at a word and finding it suddenly turn senseless under one's eyes: that can happen also to a drama if one stares at some part of it too fixedly. One would not have thought that there were problems in the burial, and of course there are none deserving of the name. But let us start gazing at this event with unnatural intensity, and some astonishing results can accrue.

For example, it has been seriously suggested that the first

[1] It is partly because of this quality that the play was, and is, so popular.

person to bury Polyneices was Ismene. (I gather my **knowledge** of this from Professor J. E. Harry.[1] Mr Harry was not the originator of the theory—he does not, in the end, endorse it; he is merely its sympathetic reviewer.) The scholar in question was led to his hypothesis by brooding over that second visit. Polyneices had been buried once—at least, all requisite dues had been paid. Why should the person responsible for those original rites have gone a second time to the scene? Only one assumption is tenable—Ismene preceded Antigone. Antigone does not visit the corpse 'a second time': she had not been there before! Ismene herself says (536) 'I have done the deed—if my sister allows me'. 'Possibly she went straight to the field after her first conversation with Antigone.' And are there not features in the burial that suggest her handiwork rather than that of her bolder, more forthright sister? There is that timid strewing of dust, for instance—does not that seem like Ismene? And if she still seems too shrinking to have done it, let us remember the courage of which the weakest women are capable when inspired by some frenzy of devotion. As for frenzy, Creon says she was frenzied. This may, of course, have been the emotional consequence of her realization of Antigone's danger; but is the other view altogether precluded? Might she not have been showing reaction—'after the tremendous nervous strain she was under when performing the act of "burying" the body'? Mr Harry, as I say, does not quite subscribe to this theory. He points out, for example, that a seemingly insuperable objection is the guard's description of Antigone's behaviour—she seemed surprised to find the body uncovered, called down curses on the doers of the deed.

[1] *Greek Tragedy* (1933), pp. 118-19.

Indeed, her behaviour impressed the guard as like a bird's when robbed of its nestlings. Mr Harry sees the force of this; all the same he says we should remember that the guard was *interpreting* the scene: perhaps he misconstrued Antigone's demeanour. Still, there is a point of linguistics to be reckoned with, and this, in Mr Harry's opinion, may be regarded as settling the matter. Ismene uses the perfect tense—'I am guilty if she consents'. She does not make an explicit assertion; if she had made one, she would have used the aorist.

Mr Harry is a notable scholar: all the more remarkable, therefore, is his patience. That he should pay such a theory the compliment of one-tenth of a second's attention—that is what a little takes one aback. And if the reader should yet have any doubts on the score of the documentary fallacy— if he is still not convinced that it exists or regards it as fuss about nothing—then I ask him to ponder the above. It would have taxed one's invention to fabricate so incredible a specimen of its working.

Yet even this view of the second burial is not quite so harmful as Dr Norwood's. Dr Norwood asks, why should there be a second burial at all? 'Why is she at first undetected yet compelled by circumstances to perform the "burial"-rites twice?'[1] (We may answer this question very easily: it is because Sophocles is writing a drama; and the first requisite of a drama is that its events shall interest and grip: Antigone must be permitted to accomplish the burial at least *once*. A moment's reflection will show what a miserable travesty of our play we should have had if she had been caught in the act the first time, with the burial not even achieved.) But this is Dr Norwood's answer: the second burial exists purely

[1] *Op. cit.*, p. 140.

and simply to remind us that the act is beyond her powers: if Creon is resolved against it 'she *cannot* "bury" Polyneices'. 'The king has posted guards, who remove the pious dust which she has scattered'—and the gruesome contest might well go on for ever. Dr Norwood's inference is that she ought never to have started it, since she cannot hope to conclude it successfully.

It is hard to reply to this briefly: one would have to go too far back, and argue about the very nature of drama— why men write it, why it exists, what it is for. I merely give it as my own conviction that while the other theory was just fantastic, this strikes at the very root of the tragedy, is a denial of its inmost spirit.

One other aspect of the burial may be mentioned: Sophocles resorts to double time, a device very useful to dramatists (their resort to it may not always be conscious). The actual events of the play are continuous—it would hardly be possible, so to say, to put a pin between them. The Argives fled in the night—it is daybreak when the action opens. The edict was promulgated shortly before dawn. In the short interval before the watch was set Antigone visited the corpse. From then on event follows event: there is no appreciable pause. But what a different impression this gives:

For the altars of our city and of our hearths have been tainted, one and all, by birds and dogs, with carrion from the hapless corpse, the son of Oedipus: and therefore the gods no more accept prayer and sacrifice at our hands, or the flame of meat-offering; nor doth any bird give a shrill cry, for they have tasted the fatness of a slain man's blood.[1]

Time in a drama is relative (as, indeed, it often is in life); it

[1] Vv. 1016-22, trans. Jebb.

can be stretched or compacted at will. The same term, measured in hours and minutes, can be induced to give very different impressions. One would say here, from the picture of Teiresias, that there had been leisure for the evil to penetrate; in truth there has hardly been leisure; it is merely Sophocles' legerdemain.

The second matter is perhaps even slighter, but raises an interesting critical principle. Teiresias has given clear warnings to Creon and these are taken up and emphasized by the Chorus—who, indeed, translate them into positive injunctions: 'Go, free the maiden from the vault, and prepare a tomb for him who lies dead.' Creon is now nearly in a panic, and makes instant preparations to obey. He bids his servants take axes and says that he is going at once to unloose her. The natural interpretation of this is that he means to make all speed to the cave. To our surprise we learn from the messenger that in fact he did nothing of the kind. He and his party made a wide detour, attending first to the burial of Polyneices; and only when those lengthy rites had been completed did they turn away towards Antigone's cavern. By then it was too late to save her. When they arrived they found her hanging and Haemon about to die.

There has been much speculation over the meaning of this. We must be clear, I think, in the first place, that—as always—it is a question of *impression*. (This may be a light-sounding word, but there is hardly another that suits.) A drama exists to make an effect, and our task is to receive that effect. Here, as ever, then, the vital thing is to yield to the impact of the drama, and not to think of the problem as an opportunity for deductive reasoning.

First, for that 'too late' arrival of Creon. Here, at the

beginning, we must distinguish. Creon, in fact, arrives too late: there is no shadow of doubt about that. But the question is always of the value that facts are accorded in a drama. Is this fact brought into relief, does the drama make capital of the lateness?

Consider this passage from *King Lear*:

> *Edmund.* I pant for life: some good I mean to do
> Despite of mine own nature. Quickly send,
> Be brief in it, to the castle; for my writ
> Is on the life of Lear and on Cordelia.
> Nay, send in time.
> *Albany.* Run, run, O run!
> *Edgar.* To who, my lord? Who hath the office? Send
> Thy token of reprieve.
> *Edmund.* Well thought on: take my sword,
> Give it the Captain.
> *Albany.* Haste thee for thy life.[1]

Surely this points the difference. Here 'too late' is a genuine motif: the effect of it is unforgettable, it is part and parcel of our experience of *King Lear*. How much milder is 'too late' in the *Antigone*. It is true that the Chorus is urgent and that Creon seems to catch the infection. But that is the end of the matter. The company takes its leisurely progress, and, though, in fact, it is two minutes late, this has not been an *issue* of the drama.

We have only to look at the sequence to see why it has to be as it is. Antigone's death is, of course, foreordained. No matter what route Creon took to the cavern he was destined to arrive too late. If he had made all the haste in the world he would still not have been in time—for that is the plan of the drama, that Antigone is to die. The question

[1] Act v, Sc. 3, ll. 243-51.

was merely, then, of the order of events, and that was a quite elementary problem. The description of the shattering events at the cave *must* come after the description of the burial rites. The reverse order, was, of course, unthinkable —the drama would have lapsed towards absurdity.

The inner reasons, then, for the sequence are plain. But how does it look from our side? It will not stand up to much critical pressure. We do not know why Creon changed his mind—or, if he did not change his mind, why he hit on the extraordinary idea of proceeding first to the body of Polyneices. The truth is that there is *no* reason—no presentable, dramatic reason. Sophocles had his own private reasons as playwright—these are clear enough technical reasons— but there is no motive within the play for the act. For it seems idle to pin it to character. Professor W. C. Greene has made the suggestion that it shows Creon once again as the extremist.[1] Before, Creon was excessive in ill-will, now he is as excessive in good. He is so bent on doing what is right that he loses all sense of reality. His conduct, unquestionably, is ironic; but this diagnosis is surely far-fetched. Mr Bowra also finds a clue in character, or at least in 'habits of thought', but the habits of thought that Mr Bowra picks out seem different from those that struck Mr Greene. 'In his warning Teiresias has spoken emphatically about the wrong done to Polyneices and not mentioned Antigone till later; the discordant birds and the unburned sacrifices are due to the unburied body; it is the denial of burial which causes the conflict with Antigone. So it takes first place in Creon's mind. He pursues his own habits of thought and fails to save Antigone or Haemon.'[2] I am not quite sure what

[1] *Moira* (1944), p. 147.   [2] *Op. cit.*, p. 111.

Mr Bowra is thinking of, but in any case he is hardly being faithful to the play. The Chorus have their minds bent on Antigone: they know that her rescue is the critical matter. Polyneices, having waited so long, can at least wait five minutes longer; the case of Antigone may be urgent. This is obviously the view of the Chorus and one must assume it to be Creon's view. It would be the view of any person of sense, and of the slightest imagination and feeling. There can be little question, then, that when he leaves, it is with the intention of going straight to the tomb: indeed, he as good as tells us that he is. Then, when he is out of our sight, some change seems to come over his ideas. We know nothing of the reasons for the change; strictly speaking, as I say, there *are* no reasons. It is purely a matter of structural convenience; and our cue is to recognize this, and not waste a thought on his motive.

The third matter is a genuine problem. Jebb rightly said of it that it 'affords one of the most interesting exercises for criticism which can be found in ancient literature'.[1]

At v. 806 Antigone enters upon a lyric interchange with the Chorus. While she is engaged in it (as I have suggested) her tone becomes somewhat stylized: we lose sight for a little of the real Antigone while this vein of poetic self-pity lasts. The tone persists even after the *commos* has ended. 'Tomb, bridal-chamber, eternal prison in the caverned rock, whither I go to find mine own, those many who have perished, and whom Persephone hath received among the dead!' Then her natural voice begins to return: by the end of the speech it is strongly back. Her lineaments come into focus again: a note of asperity—*her* note—peeps out. We recognize once more,

[1] *Sophocles: The Antigone* (1906), p. 258.

and for the last time, the Antigone-Cordelia touch: 'Nay, then, if these things are pleasing to the gods, when I have suffered my doom, I shall come to know my sin; but if the sin is with my judges, I could wish them no fuller measure of evil than they, on their part, mete wrongfully to me.' This is the authentic Antigone ring.[1]

But in the middle part of her speech she has given vent to very strange utterance. She has said something so astonishing —something so apparently unlike her and so far-fetched and grotesque in itself—that many have refused to credit Sophocles with the passage.

Here is the last speech of Antigone (square brackets enclose the portion that is suspect):

Tomb, bridal chamber, eternal prison in the caverned rock, whither I go to find mine own, those many who have perished, and whom Persephone hath received among the dead! Last of all shall I pass thither, and far most miserably of all, before the term of my life is spent. But I cherish good hope that my coming will be welcome to my father, and pleasant to thee, my mother, and welcome, brother, to thee; for, when ye died, with mine own hands I washed and dressed you, and poured drink-offerings at your graves; and now, Polyneices, 'tis for tending thy corpse that I win such recompense as this.

[And yet I honoured thee, as the wise will deem, rightly. Never, had I been a mother of children, or if a husband had been mouldering in death, would I have taken this task upon me in the city's despite. What law, ye ask, is my warrant for that word? The husband lost, another might have been found, and child from another, to replace the first-born; but, father and

---

[1] It has shown before in those taunts she addresses to Ismene. It seems a pity to try to take the sting out of these by arguing that they are not really meant, or that Antigone has an underlying purpose—to make sure that Ismene will be spared (see Jebb, *op. cit.*, p. xxix; Sheppard, *The Wisdom of Sophocles* [1947], p. 54).

mother hidden with Hades, no brother's life could ever bloom for me again. Such was the law whereby I held thee first in honour; but Creon deemed me guilty of error therein, and of outrage, ah brother mine! And now he leads me thus, a captive in his hands; no bridal bed, no bridal song hath been mine, no joy of marriage, no portion in the nurture of children; but thus forlorn of friends, unhappy one, I go living to the vaults of death.]

And what law of heaven have I transgressed? Why, hapless one, should I look to the gods any more—what ally should I invoke—when by piety I have earned the name of impious? Nay, then, if these things are pleasing to the gods, when I have suffered my doom, I shall come to know my sin; but if the sin is with my judges, I could wish them no fuller measure of evil than they, on their part, mete wrongfully to me.[1]

What an extraordinary argument to resort to! She would not have done it for a husband or a child; and she might not even have done it for a brother if there had been other living brothers in the background. Irreplaceability, that is to say, is her standard: a relative becomes important precisely in the degree in which he or she is a rarity. It is no wonder that many a reader has blinked, then tried again to make sense of the passage.

It is the fashion nowadays to take the opposite view and to count it strange that the passage should have been questioned. This seems to me a preposterous attitude. Antigone is a strong-minded woman, and all her speeches have been notable for sense. Nothing indicated that her wits were leaving her, and indeed even here she is lucid enough: only, her logic goes suddenly mad. Then she pulls herself together and is sane again. Why should we not stare in wonderment at the passage?

[1] Vv. 891-928, trans. Jebb.

We might be excused for regarding it askance even if we were unaware that there were external reasons for perhaps suspecting it. It turns out that the passage is borrowed; its original is in Herodotus. Darius formed suspicions of Intaphernes, and arrested him with his children and all his near relatives. Then there follows this story:

When all had been seized and put in chains, as malefactors condemned to death, the wife of Intaphernes came and stood continually at the palace-gates, weeping and wailing sore. So Darius after a while, seeing that she never ceased to stand and weep, was touched with pity for her, and bade a messenger go to her and say, 'Lady, king Darius gives thee as a boon the life of one of thy kinsmen—choose which thou wilt of the prisoners.' Then she pondered awhile before she answered, 'If the king grants me the life of one alone, I make choice of my brother'. Darius, when he heard the reply, was astonished, and sent again, saying, 'Lady, the king bids thee tell him why it is that thou passest by thy husband and thy children, and preferrest to have the life of thy brother spared. He is not so near to thee as thy children, nor so dear as thy husband.' She answered, 'Oh king, if the gods will, I may have another husband and other children when these are gone. But as my father and my mother are no more, it is impossible that I should have another brother. This was my thought when I asked to have my brother spared'. Then it seemed to Darius that the lady spoke well, and he gave her, besides the life that she had asked, the life also of her eldest son, because he was greatly pleased with her. But he slew all the rest.[1]

I make one or two comments first on this story. It seems odd that the wife's behaviour should ever have been thought of as life-like—and, especially, that it should ever have been believed that a mother could prefer a brother to a child

---

[1] Bk. III, ch. 119, trans. Rawlinson.

(there might, perhaps, be very exceptional cases). But it was seriously argued by Carl Robert[1] that this story reflected a cultural attitude—that in a certain given century B.C. (the fifth) mothers did, in fact, put their brothers above their children. Robert, naturally, has no evidence to offer, for the Meleager legend is not really evidence (in any case the circumstances there were exceptional: the son committed a murder; furthermore, he was mature). Nor is it proper to admit as evidence those 'quaint subtleties' (as Jebb well calls them) of Aeschylus: as when Apollo defends Orestes on the ground that a man's mother is not really his parent; or when Athena votes for Orestes because she herself has had no mother at all. What other evidence is there? I gather from anthropologists that even among native tribes no clear proof of such a thing can be found. Set a woman on the bank of a stream: suppose that her child and her brother are in it and that both are in danger of drowning. Was there ever a time in history when the woman could have saved the brother? We are not really dealing with a *Volksanschauung*; we are dealing with some basic facts of biology.

But the story in itself is enough. Robert has the extra-ordinary idea that the point of view of Herodotus coincides with the point of view of the woman: that is to say, that it is Darius who in the story is the odd one, who takes the eccentric standpoint. It is his initial attitude that is barbarous; his later conclusion that 'the woman spoke well' represents his conversion to what (at that time) was normal Greek feeling on the matter. And the narrator must concur in this view: otherwise he would have been obliged to criticize it.

One hardly knows what to say; anyone who cannot *see*

[1] *Op. cit.*, vol. I, p. 333.

that it is not this kind of story would not, of course, be open to argument on the point; but one might perhaps risk the assertion that, if it *had* been this kind of story, then its flatness and general insipidity would have prevented its surviving five minutes. What would have been the point of telling such a story if the woman's decision had been merely ordinary? The only conceivable point would have lain in the ignorance of Darius—in the fact that outsiders existed who were unaware of the true doctrine of this matter, and whose eyes were occasionally opened. The story is very ancient and widespread; does anyone imagine that its enduring quality could have been derived from a point like that? It is obvious of course, that it exists for the paradox. It lives because it is surprising, because it tickles the fancy with its strangeness. That is precisely why it came into being, because it reports an oddity in life. The wife's reply has a certain aptness that Antigone's remarks in the play have not, but it is merely the aptness of an epigram expressed in terms of human behaviour. She ponders for a while on her problem, then out she comes with this answer that knocks Darius all of a heap. What she says is not for a moment believable, but that does not detract from its piquancy. It is the ingenuity of her reasoning, her startling, paradoxical logic, that gives the salt to the story and assures it of long survival. It has, of course, exactly the tang of some fairy tales.

So much for the Herodotean anecdote. What, next, of this strange echo of it in Antigone's speech? Does it harmonize with its new context? Can one relate it to one's imaginings of Antigone? I will put briefly the chief considerations as I see them.

(1). It is sometimes said that Antigone acted purely

from feeling and that this speech shows her struggling to express what she had never before been able to put into words: that it is her attempted formulation of what had been the instinctive dictates of her heart. Naturally the formulation is clumsy and does little justice to what had really been moving her.

I do not think that this is an accurate statement. I do not think it is even true to say, with Mr Sheppard, that 'her resolve sprang from an impulse of pure love, not from a calculation or a sense of duty to the family or even a religious scruple'.[1] This is an incomplete description. Naturally it is her love which most impresses us at the outset, but as early as v. 77 she is speaking of the guilt of dishonouring 'that which is honoured in the sight of the gods'. It is *all* there, clear in her mind. 'Antigone has no reasons; she has only her instinct.'[2] On the contrary, she has very good reasons and has been able to express them excellently. That is what so struck Goethe, that Antigone throughout the course of the play had been so lucid in her accounts of her conduct, and then, at the end, should put forward a motive 'which is quite unworthy of her and which almost borders on the comic'. Deep down, no doubt, her attitude is instinctive. She feels an overmastering imperative and is no more capable than another of a thoroughly reasoned justification, but she justifies herself as far as she can. She reverts again and again to the laws, to the 'unwritten statutes of heaven'; she feels that she is answerable somehow to the gods, and she is able to express this feeling. She has been capable of formulations. She has drawn most lucid contrasts between the compulsions directing her conduct and the

[1] *Op. cit.*, p. 53.   [2] Gilbert Norwood, *op. cit.*, p. 139.

justice to which Creon pays homage. How is it, then, that the clear-minded Antigone should suddenly lose all her clarity: should unexpectedly desert her ground and plunge into these nonsensical paradoxes about husbands and brothers and children?

(2). This brings us to the contention of a breakdown. Does her courage suddenly leave her? Or, in the stress of her situation does her mind lose something of its grip? Does she feel herself at last in an obscurity, when she cannot be confident of anything? Do we see her, in these strange lines, groping pathetically in the dark for a foothold?

This can seem a very plausible view—until we look once again at the text. Where are the signs of the coming on of this breakdown? And why is it that she recovers so swiftly? Nothing is more important to note than that Antigone *resumes* her distinctive manner. It is easy, in discussing the passage, to give the impression that the uncertain, faltering, confused Antigone is the last Antigone we see. 'As the end draws near her defences fail one by one, until, in that marvellously moving and tragic speech which was not to the taste of those who saw in Antigone chiefly a martyr to the Higher Law, she abandons everything except the fact that she did it and had to do it.'[1] Not at all: in her *final* words she has abandoned nothing: she is completely the Antigone we knew. She is a bitter Antigone, of course, but all of her courage is there. She is clear, unperplexed, defiant. The Chorus recognize the old note: 'Still the same tempest of the soul vexes this maiden with the same fierce gusts.'[2] The problem is to harmonize this Antigone with the Antigone of a few seconds before.

[1] H. D. F. Kitto, *op. cit.*, p. 127.   [2] Vv. 929-30, trans. Jebb.

(3). It is not legitimate to paraphrase the passage, and in so doing smooth down its roughnesses. It is the easiest matter in the world to give an account of it that sounds quite unexceptionable: to suggest that, of course, she is leaving out certain links in her reasoning, that she is assuming this and that and the other, and that what she is really meaning to say is as follows. Our concern is with what she says. As Jebb acutely remarked of Bellermann: 'Bellermann's subtlety invests the crude and blunt sophistry of the text with an imaginative charm which is not its own.'[1] This critical process still persists. Take, for instance, Mr Bowra's account:

So we may wonder why Sophocles used the Herodotean theme. The answer is surely that he wished to display the special character of Antigone's devotion to Polyneices. She compares him with the husband who is not hers, with children who are not yet born. In her life her love for Polyneices is the strongest tie she has known. It is a reality like nothing else, deeply rooted in the sense of kinship which means so much to her. She considers what she might have done, and decides that only for a brother would she have taken so great a risk and incurred so heavy a penalty. She could have neglected her brother and lived safely with Haemon. She has chosen otherwise, to satisfy her love for her brother at the cost of her life. If we take her words as they come, they are deeply touching and perfectly natural.[2]

I do not think that even so Mr Bowra comes within reach of proving his point. Is it really natural for Antigone to declare that only for a brother would she have done these things?

[1] *Op. cit.*, p. 262. Professor R. E. Wycherley (*Classical Philology*, XLII [1947], p. 51) contends that Jebb falls into the same trap himself in his translation of lines 74-5: that Antigone's reasoning at this point has a 'crudity' that Jebb by his 'elegant translation' removes. I cannot feel that the discrepancy here is very serious.

[2] *Op. cit.*, p. 95.

But the paraphrase sufficiently softens the passage; Antigone's words come to us muffled through Mr Bowra's rephrasing; we are made to miss the keen impact of their discords. But these discords are essential in the problem. Would Antigone have expressed herself so? That is the core of the question. Would such comparisons ever have occurred to her, do they strike us as in any way like her? That is what we have to decide.

A confident decision is, of course, not to be thought of. The matter would be very different if evidence of diction and metre were conclusive. As it is, the most we can do is to assess the probabilities as we see them, and be content to leave the truth in uncertainty.

Aristotle accepted the passage as by Sophocles and expressed only mild bewilderment. He noted Antigone's declaration (that she would have defied the city *only* for a brother) as the kind of oddity in a drama that the dramatist is under an obligation to account for. Aristotle points out that Sophocles has satisfactorily fulfilled this duty. Apparently, then, Aristotle swallowed Antigone's explanation without trouble. (We must remember, in his excuse, that he was preoccupied just here with theory. In any case Aristotle's critical wits were not invariably at full stretch.)

The grotesqueness of it cannot be blinked. Was Sophocles capable of writing it? Could the topsy-turvy dialectic have made, in itself, a strong appeal to his fancy? And could he have succumbed to the temptation to thrust it in, knowing that it would never really have time to jar?

The latter point, I think, is clear. It has been admirably made by Professor D. L. Page.[1] The lines would occupy, in

[1] *Actors' Interpolations in Greek Tragedy* (1934), p. 89.

speaking, just a second or two: and 'he would be a remark-ably acute spectator who, hearing these lines spoken for the first time, rapidly too and with great passion, divined then and there the weakness and incongruity'. Mr Page adds: 'I suggest that no spectator was ever offended by the incongruity of these verses, when he heard them suddenly spoken on the stage in the middle of this speech.' I do not think this opinion can be questioned.

What it means is that *either* Sophocles or an interpolating actor could have inserted the passage without very great risk: which it was, each must decide for himself, for the answer will be a reflection of his whole view and impression of Sophocles. But the purely critical question seems clear. The lines do not fit Antigone: only by sophistry can they be made to do so. If Sophocles really wrote them, then either he lost, for these few seconds, his grip (was striving for something we cannot quite see), or he observed the chance for this rather piquant effect, and thought the lapse from truth no great harm.

CHAPTER VIII

DRAMA OF DRAMAS:
THE *OEDIPUS TYRANNUS*

POSSIBLY the best service a critic can render the *Oedipus Tyrannus* is to leave it alone. The next best service is to seek to recover it; and the direction in which any such attempt must be made is fairly clear. The *Oedipus Tyrannus* is a very great play. It is so great a play that we are a little unwilling to believe that it could fall short, if rightly examined, of *any* of those attributes that a great tragedy might be expected to possess. Tradition has built up a list of such attributes, and criticism of the *Oedipus Tyrannus* consists largely in the effort to demonstrate that the play, if only we adopt the right point of view, really does square with every conceivable demand that could be made of it. One understands and to some extent sympathizes with the motives that underlie such criticism; yet it can only do the play a wrong. The *Oedipus Tyrannus* is so consummate in its kind that we need not pain ourselves to adjust it to any preconceived ideal of what a drama should be. By improving it we can only hurt it. Let us accept the *Oedipus Tyrannus*, with gratitude, as it is.

In an attempt to strip from the play its chief disguises let us begin with the view that it is a drama of character. It is easy to understand the powerful critical compulsions behind such a view. A tragedy without character is unthinkable, and to concede that, in a play so famous, character could have smaller importance than plot is to commit something like a grotesquerie. That Oedipus possesses a character is certain. It is not very clearly defined. It reaches us through a set of acts so few and so exceptional that we cannot estimate it very surely; but it is there. Oedipus is brave, energetic, resourceful, confident, impetuous. He is not outstandingly of the reflective type (it is odd that he should have untangled the riddle). He does not possess, as far as we can make out, an intelligence of piercing quickness or very remarkable reach. But he has at least an average mind, and he is beyond the average in his resolution and valour. In the visible action of the play we are made to see his faults as well as his virtues. He is too precipitate. It seems difficult for him, when excited, to hold more than one thing before his gaze at a time, so that he rushes into actions that are absurdly ill-judged, and that could be very dangerous for himself in their consequences. His treatment of Teiresias and Creon is grossly unfair and is based on suspicions that are almost childish. All this is true. Yet when we examine his conduct in the past—the conduct that, by degrees, has brought him to this ruin—do we find in it very much to criticize? He was living happily in Corinth, the son (as he thought) of Polybus and Merope, until a chance encounter brought into his mind a doubt and a worry. A roisterer at a banquet shouted to him: 'You are not really your father's son.' He questioned his parents. They did their best to reassure him, but rumours continued to spread and he could not dismiss the matter from his mind. In the end he went, for his own satisfaction, to Delphi. The result was surprising and distracting. He was disappointed in the knowledge he sought, but received in its place dire warnings of other woes to come. He was fated, he learnt, to defile his mother's bed and to become the slayer of his father. Shocked, he decided there and then to put miles between himself and his country.

So far, what can fairly be said against him? We should be careful how we pose the problem. It is not quite proper to put the question in this form: whether a man of another character would have acted differently. The question is rather this: whether the character of Oedipus can reasonably be charged with his downfall—whether, in a sufficiently emphatic and pointed way, it can be seen as the source of his troubles. The question, in familiar phrase, is whether he brought his misfortunes on his own head. (In the *Trachiniae* there was something of a parallel.) It may be conceded readily that there are certain types of people who would have solved the problem of Oedipus in an instant —cunning people who, hearing what he heard, would have fended off calamity for ever. Uriah Heep would certainly have done so—Destiny would have been no match for Heep. One can imagine other types of men, pigeon-livered and lacking in gall, who would have rushed forthwith into a hermitage or taken to the desert spaces. It is easy to think of any number of effective rejoinders to the formulated threats of the oracle—the simplest would have been plain suicide. But all this is rather beside the point and does not prove that Oedipus, in a human way of speaking, was ill-advised in the line he took. Critics who stand or fall by character adopt curious manoeuvres here. Some[1] have as good as said that if Oedipus had been a more lackadaisical person he would have found himself in no trouble at all, for if he had been endowed

[1] For example, Mr Kitto, *op. cit.*, p. 140.

with a carefree character he would not, in the first place, have been stung by the taunt; in that case, he would not have questioned his parents, he would not have resorted to the oracle, he would not, therefore, have found himself at the cross-roads, and the later disasters would not have had a chance to develop. This is a very neat illustration of the absurdities that sometimes follow from believing that, in every play worth its salt, we simply must show that 'character is destiny'. In strict aesthetics this, no doubt, ought to be so, but in fact we do not always see it. The implication of the view just mentioned is that Oedipus pays a price for being normal. He suffers because he has natural feelings, because he is a man who is fond of his parents and who likes to think that his social status is respected; because he has enough initiative and energy to try to find out the truth for himself. There was nothing extraordinary in his action; in view of the persistent rumours it was natural for him to be worried, natural to consult the oracle. (In similar circumstances to-day he would have visited some office of records.) It is true that he is not acute. The oracle leaves him with a difficult problem. He does not sit down like a chess-player and ponder his retort to all possible moves. If he had, it would possibly have struck him that the man who jeered at the banquet might just conceivably have been speaking the truth. Suppose Polybus and Merope were not really his parents; then he will not be securing himself by abandoning Corinth but will be rushing into unknown perils. But the oracle has placed the emphasis so cunningly that Oedipus does not appear to us to be stupid; nor, in plain fact, would acuteness have helped him. The oracle would not answer his question directly, but it *seemed* to warn him against the direst dangers at Corinth, and there was no reason why he should think it malevolent. If we imagine ourselves in his situation we must see that he is forced to make a plunge in the dark. He cannot *know* who is speaking the truth, or how much of the truth is being spoken. As he is a man of normal impulses who wishes to proceed with his life, all he can do is to make a guess. He plumps for what seems the right course of action, and this course is assuredly as reasonable as another.

What, next, of the affray at the cross-roads? Here, again, many men would have eluded the peril. (Sir Andrew Aguecheek, for one, would have eluded it.) Oedipus is, no doubt, impetuous. The indignities to which he is subjected sting him, and in a moment or two he has 'slain them all'. Looking down on this affair from our vantage point it is not difficult for us to see that Oedipus' behaviour was rash. If he had been eminently of the planning type he would long before this have compiled a handlist of everything that he must not do; and would have so wisely drilled himself that it would have been almost automatic to refrain. But again, let us remember his assumptions, and the appearance that the drama gives to these happenings. A novel might have made a point of his folly; the mere fact is that the play does not. Simply, he has not yet seriously thought that his father could be any other than Polybus. He knows no reason why his parents should have lied, nor has the oracle suggested that they did; the *suggestion* of the oracle is otherwise. So he runs into the terrible trap; but trap, surely, is the right word to use. It is true that he has been somewhat impetuous; it is true that he has been less than supremely reflective. He has not triple-plated himself against Destiny, has not been alert for every possible ambush. Equally, Destiny has not played fair. To say, of his conduct so far, that 'his destiny lay in himself' is merely to do obeisance to a shibboleth. It caricatures the struggle. That cunning, relentless enmeshment, that ruthless, secret campaign—what chance has he had against this? To talk of him as deciding his fate is to distort this picture to absurdity, to burlesque what so clearly has been happening.

The deed at the cross-roads was unfortunate; so was his marriage with the widow of Laius; marriage, also, should have been on his black list. But, again, we must not consider this in the abstract; it is the impression of the drama that counts. We do not feel that he was inexcusably rash—do not feel that he was very injudicious. Let us remind ourselves once more of his case. He has heard certain bodeful things; it is obvious that he must take care. Well, he has made his dispositions—dispositions that, in all the circumstances, are logical and reasonably safe. We have no right, as we read this drama, to blame him for taking *some* risks. (Indeed, as we read the drama, there is not the slightest temptation to blame him; the blame comes later—in criticism—when we have a little withdrawn from the play.) He feels, and is justified in feeling, that he has taken fair measures of security; to have made the security absolute would have meant resigning himself to a half-life; more accurately, perhaps, it would have meant a retirement from life *in toto*. He prefers to accept that margin of danger, and, with moderate luck, all would have been well. He fails because of the odds against him. Who would have thought that out of ten million women Jocasta was the one foreordained for his undoing? It is the feeling of these *odds* against Oedipus that is the essential feeling of the drama.

And that is why insistence on character seems to me at every point a mistake. It is a truly damaging mistake, because it amounts to a kind of blasphemy against the special greatness of this play. It seeks to depress that greatness and bring another sort of greatness to the front. Critics feel that they must deprecate plot—that to do otherwise is a kind of betrayal, is being somehow false to their charge. So the tenor of the argument is often that, though the plot (needless to say) is wonderful, the *Oedipus Tyrannus* does not depend on it. (One expects constantly to meet the explicit assertion that the play could have done quite as well without it.) At any rate, it is 'overridden', is, when all is said, an 'accessory'.[1] 'In the *Tyrannus*,' says Mr Webster, 'the story is still important and exciting'[2] but is not, he implies, the main business; there are higher glories than the story, more respectable merits than the mere plot. If I may repeat without offence what I have said, there is a kind of blasphemy in such sayings. To disparage the plot of the *Oedipus Tyrannus*—a play that is plot *in excelsis!* Here is one of the supreme stories of the world—and we speak, apologetically, of the story! Of course there is character in the play—without character there could not be plot. But to make of this plot a subsidiary thing!—it seems to me a critical malfeasance.

But perhaps there is some other way of rescuing the drama from the deep damnation of dependence on plot. What, for example, of the religious strain? Can we find a profound 'moral insight'? Is there some 'eternal' significance in the tragedy?

Mr Bowra has a generalized theory of the nature of the

---

[1] H. D. F. Kitto, *op. cit.*, p. 138.   [2] *Op. cit.*, p. 169.

Sophoclean plays. He thinks that they are essentially plays about the relation between gods and men. It is not so much men and men as men and gods who are in conflict. There exists a 'divine will' for men; for various reasons men oppose it, and the plays show them paying the penalty.

I feel quite sure, for my own part, that as a generalized theory this will not do. Without twisting the obvious facts, how can the *Antigone* be brought within it? We know where right lies in the *Antigone*; in that sense we know where the gods stand. To some extent they indicate their feelings, and they make their weight felt indirectly in the action. But the contest that we hear and feel is the contest between Antigone and Creon. Or, for another example, take the *Electra*. Mr Bowra says, 'Electra fights for the gods even at the cost of much spiritual damage to herself'.[1] This may be true in part. (I am doubtful of the extent of the spiritual damage; this seems to me largely the creation of critics.) But grant that Electra fights for the right—fights, if we like, for the gods; does this mean that the play we see is a conflict between gods and men? That is just to reject the visible play, to brush it aside for what we think is its import. It is the very mark of Sophoclean drama that the conflicts it presents are human; to speak of these human conflicts as if they were, after all, subordinate issues—as if their chief value were to lead us to the veritable matters behind them—surely this is like abolishing drama. The human conflicts are not concessions, mere sops to our thirst for an action; they are the stuff of which plays are made.

I do not think, then, that Mr Bowra's theory can hold; one merely has to look at the plays to see that he is not describing

[1] *Op. cit.*, p. 366.

them truly. But the *Oedipus Tyrannus* might seem, at first sight, the one exception; it is certainly, of all the plays, the one to which Mr Bowra's theory applies most nearly. Here, for once, there is certainly a suggestion of a conflict between a man and the gods. There are invisible Powers in the background and there is a secret game that they are playing; our consciousness of all this is intense. Oedipus has quarrels in the course of the drama; he is in conflict with this person and that. But no human being is his enemy; his enemy is this malevolent Unknown. Here, for once, Mr Bowra's pattern seems to fit; here one man is in conflict with the gods.

The question is, then, of the meaning. Has Sophocles a deep design? Is he trying to tell us something about the nature of man and the universe? If he is, then assuredly we must listen; and, if we find that he has some such Truth to communicate, we must be prepared to revise our impressions. Plot, then, will lose some of its lustre. Great as the play is as pure story, we cannot claim that the story is paramount if there is this Truth underlying the action.

There is only one way, of course, to answer the question and that is to examine the play; and we must examine the play *by itself*. If there were really a pattern of tragedy in Sophocles, then we should be justified in looking for it here. If the other six plays were so uniform that we could say with reasonable confidence, 'this is the kind of thing that you find in Sophocles, this is the pattern that life bears to his eyes', then we should expect to light on this pattern. But no such uniformity exists. Nothing prohibits us from approaching the *Oedipus Tyrannus* with a perfectly open mind; and nothing ought to make us uneasy if we were to find it in some respects unique.

I think that in some respects it is really exceptional—that while the other plays show various resemblances, this one stands apart from them all.

For example, Mr Bowra affirms that 'for Sophocles the tragic issue arises in some breach in the divine order of the world'.[1] Sophocles' heroes 'have resisted their destinies'[2] and it is for this ignorance or stubbornness that they are humbled. Such formulae sound moderately plausible and may seem justified in this play or that. But how are we to apply them to the *Oedipus Tyrannus*? 'Men who have resisted their destinies.' Has Oedipus resisted his destiny? He has heard his awful destiny announced. He most certainly has not rushed to fulfil it; he has strained every nerve to avoid it. Does this mean, then, that he has committed a wrong In his case can the formula mean *anything*? Mr Bowra says that in Sophocles a man cannot hope for salvation until he has learned the ultimate wisdom that he must 'do what the gods demand'.[3] In its application to Oedipus is there even a grain of sense in this dictum? Oedipus has fled from his destiny, has tried frantically to elude his Pursuer, only to find, like a coursed hare, that his every move has been countered, and that every exit has been cunningly blocked. What affinity has a picture like this with the sort of tragedy that Mr Bowra is discussing—in which men learn the virtues of obedience and are taught to renounce their illusions? Oedipus has no illusions—except those that the gods have enforced on him. He certainly 'sees the truth' in the end, but has he ever tried not to see it? He would have given his soul to have seen it. We must admit that he is like other heroes in that he learns his own insignificance; that lesson is

[1] *Op. cit.*, p. 380.   [2] *Ibid.*, p. 366.   [3] *Ibid.*, p. 365.

fully brought home. But how obvious it is that there is no parallel between the tragic problem he faces and those problems that Mr Bowra has in mind! He is confronted with a dreadful future; the sins he is doomed to commit are such as gods and men will execrate. If these deeds are ever performed, then the divine order will certainly be broken; but he is the very last who wishes it broken. In Mr Bowra's view, the tragic conflict arises because 'someone has gone too far and upset the ordered harmony of life'.[1] Well, who is it who has gone too far? It is the gods who have gone too far. What real point is there in saying that 'the evil caused by the innocent Oedipus is little less than that caused by Clytaemnestra'?[2] The gods have caused Oedipus to cause it. The spectacle that this play presents is that of a man fleeing blindly from evil, and of hands reaching out to catch him and clutch him and force him to do it. When he has done evil he is polluted; he understands that thoroughly and accepts the taboo. But these gods whose cry is for order, what specimens of hypocrisy they are if they impute the disorder that has arisen to their victim; and how muddled must be Sophocles' thinking if that is the view he himself takes —if that is the way he *reads* this drama of his own creation!

It is better not to believe it. As I say, we are under no compulsion to make this play accord with a scheme; the situation will not be desperate if we should in the end have found no formula to fit it. Better to leave the play nakedly unclassified than to tug and strain at the formulae in a vain effort to induce them to cover it. How much tugging and straining is needed Mr Bowra, I think, has sufficiently exhibited. Or take the problems that arise in the sequel.

[1] *Op. cit.*, p. 380. [2] *Ibid.*, p. 381.

The play shows Oedipus at bay. As the dread coincidences multiply he refuses for a long while to see. If we cast about for reasons for this slowness we can put forward this 'fault' or that to explain it. We can say, for example, that he is proud. That, indeed, is what Mr Bowra says: Oedipus has 'a kingly pride and high spirit which prevents him from seeing the truth'.[1] Other tragic heroes have 'passions' that 'over-power their sense of reality', and this we may take to be Oedipus' passion. So once more we succeed in bringing him into a scheme. A little later, however, the position is different. Presently, the truth is just beyond the edge of his conscious-ness, and the sense of this makes him restive. He has seemed to hang back from seeing the truth, now he strives forward in the effort to see it. All who are round him are frightened; they beg him to question no further. If he had stopped short at this point—if, surmising some horror in the offing, he had come to a lightning decision and resolved to let everything rest—then, conceivably, all would have been well. (We do not know, of course, what the gods would have done; it is hard to think that they would have taken defeat quite so easily.) Oedipus, in any case, is not that kind of a man. He feels, of a sudden, hemmed in and responds by pressing outwards for air. He has the nobility to *wish* to know, to be resolute to put the matter to the test; let the frame of things disjoint, he'll find out what these secrets are. So again, he is 'proud' and 'high-spirited', though now with an opposite result. Before, his pride made him slow, now it makes him too quick. He was in fault for not perceiving the truth; now he is in fault because he is too urgent to see it. Whatever he does, Oedipus cannot escape from his critics; the formulae

[1] *Op. cit.*, p. 373.

have him enmeshed; he can act in contrary ways, but every act betrays tragic passion. The lesson of these contradictions is clear; it is simply that the proportions in such criticism are all wrong. The play is not about the faults of Oedipus. It may be conceded that he has his failings, but these are merely incidental to the pattern. Bluntly, in the *Oedipus Tyrannus* the hero's faults are of little account. The play is too busy with another thing—with another all-powerful impression; and in the shadow of this other impression the hero's deficiencies fade into nothingness.

But what, again, of the gods? What moral can be read into their doings? What Truth does the drama enshrine? I would suggest that if critics answered this question immediately after they asked it they would often hesitate and waver. But between the asking of the question and the answering of it much elaborate discussion often intervenes, so that the shock of the answer is cushioned. Mr Bowra, for example, begins in this way: 'Sophocles' play is so grand and so tragic that it is easy to misinterpret his fundamental ideas'[1]—easy to find explanations for the downfall of Oedipus that are not really Sophocles' at all. Such a statement seems quite impeccable. We respond in instant sympathy and put ourselves into a condition of readiness. *A priori*, nothing could seem more likely than that so grand and tragic a play should have treasures of meaning to reveal. If Mr Bowra intends presently to uncover them we shall be all eyes to see what comes forth. 'A story like this can hardly fail to invite some kind of explanation, and it is legitimate to look for Sophocles'. The tragic collapse of Oedipus cries for comment or justification.'[2] Again we give provisional

---

[1] *Op. cit.*, p. 163.   [2] *Ibid.*

155

assent. We agree that it is by no means improbable that Sophocles had ideas on the subject; and when Mr Bowra goes on to assert confidently that he had, we at least wait eagerly to hear.

Then follow a dozen or so pages of discussion, at the end of which Mr Bowra is ready with his answer; and this is what he finds in the play: '*King Oedipus* shows the humbling of a great and prosperous man by the gods. This humbling is not deserved; it is not a punishment for insolence, nor in the last resort is it due to any fault of judgment or character in the man. The gods display their power because they will.'[1] In between question and answer there have intervened, as I say, a dozen pages full of very interesting commentary. But there, at the beginning, was the naked question, and here is the naked answer.

Mr Bowra has one more thing to add. The gods act 'because they will', but at least they accomplish something; they give man 'a salutary lesson',[2] and with this we reach bedrock at last. There is nothing deeper in the play than this, we are at the end of explanation, this is the ultimate moral of the drama. It seems, to speak bluntly, a fiasco. The meaning that had to be probed for, all the care to keep on the track, the patient following of clues, the rejection of inadequate hypotheses—to find this at the end of the search! We have trusted Sophocles, for this! I do not think there is the slightest immoderation in suggesting that, in that case, Sophocles has been wasting our time. It would have been far better, for all concerned, if we had never once thought of a significance. That a member of humankind should be put through such sufferings as these for no other ascertainable

[1] *Op. cit.*, p. 175. [2] *Ibid.*

reason than that he and we should learn to be modest—
should be warned (as Mr Bowra expresses it) not to be
confident, should be made to feel less secure!—it seems
altogether too much. Yet that, apparently, is the sum total of
the meaning; that is the 'fundamental idea' that we sought
for, that is the last word on the story. It is clear, of course,
that we need never have sought for it, for this is precisely
what is said in the tag, 'Count no man happy till dead'
(in other words, 'we never know what may happen, do not
be too sure of your luck, life has its ups and downs, there is
many a terrible fall—take note how all these truths are
illustrated in the story of Oedipus!'). Mr Bowra at least
concedes that 'after the hideous and harrowing events this
finale . . . may seem a little tame'.[1] Tame is assuredly the
word. It is completely and utterly negligible—a flourish at
the end of a letter, a piece of scrollwork absently drawn; a
few perfunctory words to signal that the play is over, hardly
meant to be listened to but to be drowned in the rustle of
departure.

But what of the gods themselves? With what credit do
they emerge? Of course with no credit at all. They have
picked out a man to humble him, not because he deserves to
be humbled, but in order that he may be an example to
others. Oedipus is to be taught his utter insignificance so
that mankind in general may be chastened. There is no proof
that mankind needs chastening; nothing is offered to suggest
that man needs this particular rod. Simply, the gods have
taken a whim to chasten. And yet Mr Bowra finds it possible
to say that 'Sophocles shirks none of these difficulties'.[2]
Sophocles, I would suggest, knew well that he could not

---

[1] *Op. cit.*, p. 175.   [2] *Ibid.*, p. 185.

afford even to look at them; it was more than his play was worth to allow these difficulties two seconds of attention. *Nothing* can excuse the gods, and Sophocles knew it perfectly well. That is why, in this play, he eschews thinking—why he makes no effort to explain, why he keeps so clear of philosophical embroilment, why he is so careful to allow nothing to divert him from the one thing with which he is concerned: that one thing being, of course, the writing of drama.

The theories so far discussed may be described as attempts at normalization. If it could be shown that this play was a tragedy of character, or if it could be shown that some profound religious truth underlay it, critics would feel much easier about its indisputable greatness. The greatness would seem better based; and no doubt it would, in fact, be so. But nothing whatever is to be gained by forcing the play into a pattern. It has its own wonderful quality; we only disguise and injure this quality when we try to turn it into another.

There have been various other attempts to bring the play into closer alignment with a type. For example, critics may shy from religion and may deprecate the use of the word 'explain'. To many, as to Mr Sheppard, it has seemed on the whole safer to admit that Sophocles has no solution to offer —that he is not claiming to hold the key of the riddle. The evil is there, he presents it, and with that his obligation is ended. He does not seek, like Aeschylus, to justify it; and he has none of the presumption of Euripides, who dared to challenge the powers who caused it. Sophocles is relatively detached. But critics are not quite content to stop at this point. Sophocles may be reserved and dispassionate, but after all it should be possible to show that he too had his thoughts about the universe. He may not tell us much about the gods, but what of the nature of things—has he not something to tell us about that? The nature of things is the cue. Let us suppose that the hero is not just *Oedipus*, a mere man who for inscrutable reasons has been picked out for special attention by the gods. Let us suppose that he stands for something—'human suffering' will conveniently do. Let us also depersonalize the gods—treat them a little abstractly by referring rather to the 'universe of circumstance as it is'. Immediately the play seems lifted; once more a new dignity accrues. It is unnecessary to argue for a thesis, we need not maintain that the play makes a point; but to have embodied human suffering—there already is an achievement. To have given dramatic expression to the universe of circumstance as it is—no work accomplishing that could be thought of as destitute of content.

This is a neat manoeuvre, but quite as illegitimate, in my opinion, as the others. It is just one more way of smuggling significance into the *Oedipus Tyrannus*; just one more expression of the feeling that this work, by hook or by crook, must be made to mean something; just another attempt to prove that the work really is universal. But the action of this play is exceptional; no argument can alter that. Oedipus is a world-wonder in his suffering, in his peculiar destiny he is a freak. He is a man selected out of millions to undergo this staggering fate; that is why his story is so fascinating. It fascinates because it is rare; because on any rational assessment his story—as far as we are concerned—is impossible. We can imagine it all so vividly, we can live in every one of his emotions; yet we should as reasonably fear to be hit by a thunderbolt as to be embroiled in his particular set of misfortunes. And if Oedipus, by the extreme rarity of his destiny, is outside the common lot of mankind, so is the special malignance that strikes him a thing quite apart from the universe of circumstance as it is. Circumstance has its practical jokes and its sinister-seeming moods, but a concatenation of malevolences on this scale is an absolutely unparalleled thing. The gods who really do stand for circumstance are very much milder beings and need cause no great affright. That is why it is so misleading to reduce this play to the normal. Mr Sheppard says that the dramatist is 'facing the facts',[1] and that he is asking his audience to face them; Sophocles' 'work as a tragedian is to face the facts of life'. No doubt many tragedians do this—do recognize this as their task; and it may be that in some other tragedies Sophocles himself is facing the facts; but not in the *Oedipus Tyrannus*. Here the terror of sheer coincidence is vital; to suppress that terror here is to rob the play of its essence. We have here a chain of events so abnormal that they edge into the sphere of the miraculous. We have no feeling here of the nature of things; what we feel is an *interference* with nature. The play quintessentializes misfortune; it is an epigram in ill-luck.

It is a pity to spoil this quality by damping down the abnormal; and so, I think, with lesser matters, we should be careful in our strivings for naturalism, for even in details it is easy to do harm. For example, it is dangerous to tinker with the joinery-work of the plot. All words of praise seem drab for the plot of the *Oedipus Tyrannus*: there is, of course, nothing in Sophocles to match it, nothing that comes within

[1] *The Oedipus Tyrannus of Sophocles* (1920), p. xl.

hail of it. But its extraordinary cleanness of line was not won without finesse. We must not make unfair exactions, or sight the work from improper angles. There is that recapitulation early in the play—the passage of question and answer by which we are reminded of past events. It is somewhat naïve technique, especially as the questioner has to be Oedipus, and no matter how it is managed plausibility can hardly be saved. I have already suggested[1] that we risk making things worse if we try to square the absurdities of this passage with the demands of realistic psychology. To explain such a sequence as this is, quite strictly, to tamper with the drama, for the last thing that Sophocles desired was that we should pause and test the passage. He knew (none better) its hollowness; he does not wish us to knock on it and sound it and then set about trying to strengthen it; he wishes us to hurry along. As I have said, what he is really proposing is a tacit agreement: if we will concede him this slight improbability then he undertakes to economize in his workmanship. After all, neither Sophocles nor the reader wishes to dally over expository details, but somewhere a place must be found for these basic preparatory facts. The earlier they are mentioned the better; and on the whole the simplest method (certainly the one that wastes least time) is to put them in the form of question and answer. So Oedipus suddenly becomes very dull. He admits to having heard tell of his predecessor, but for the rest is vagueness itself. There is no real way to explain this; but if we merely make that slight concession at the outset we can take all the difficulties in our stride.

It is much the same in some later sequences where the hero's reactions are rather slower than life. Bit by bit the

[1] See pp. 92 ff.

evidence gathers, and Oedipus is in the position of one who is suddenly involved in a grim intelligence test. His performance is far from outstanding. Yet by hypothesis he is an anxious man. Recent years have perhaps lulled his fears, but it would be natural to imagine that they are still there, quiescent. One would expect that at the slightest warning his whole being would become quiveringly intent. Instead, his wits seem flaccid; he lags noticeably in putting two and two together. The pattern of the truth eludes him until every last thread is in place. I do not think that the unlikelihood is important. Once again we make a slight concession, and the power of the action is so great that any check of this sort becomes trifling. But the situation is the same as before in that no good is done by explaining. Jocasta, scoffing at oracles, gives Oedipus a proof of their shallowness; it was foretold of Laius that he should die by the hand of his child; in fact, he was killed by robbers; and the child was not three days old when it was put out to perish on a mountain, with its ankles pinned together. Ankles pinned together! Oedipus hears these words, and yet, strangely, they give him no hint, start no associations moving in his mind. He harks back to what Jocasta said about cross-roads—that has set deep memories a-tremble. Mr Sheppard says that this is in character; Oedipus 'becomes absorbed with any idea which seizes him, and neglects for the moment every other thought'.[1] No doubt he is a man rather like that; yet I do not think that the explanation is sufficient; there is still some oddity left. The plain truth is that Oedipus has to be slow—rather slower than any quirk of temperament will account for. Quick wits would have meant no drama, and Sophocles is

[1] *Op. cit.*, p. 148.

again finessing. We do not much notice the slowness; it is only when we reflect that we perceive how strange it is that Oedipus should pass over these clues. So, later, the Corinthian messenger declares that Polybus was not really his father; it was this messenger himself who found Oedipus and carried him, a babe, to Corinth. And where was it, precisely, he found him? 'In the folded vales of Cithaeron.' Cithaeron! But again he fails to take the import of the word. He is brooding now on the question of his birth—fears it may turn out to be servile. He follows this blind alley of thought while Jocasta has already leapt to the truth. Again, character will not fully suffice; we are dealing with dramatic finesse.

Finally, if one examines the play one comes across many little adjustments that make for smoothness of line, though by canons of meticulous realism most of them would be hard to defend. Some are beautifully concealed. How many readers check at what Jocasta says about the servant in vv.758-60? Oedipus has learnt from her that there was one survivor from that affray at the cross-roads; it was he, of course, who brought the tidings; and Oedipus naturally wishes to know where this most important witness may be found. 'Is he now in the house?' he asks. Jocasta replies that he is not; she says that as soon as he arrived from the cross-roads 'and saw thee in possession of the kingdom' some strange fear or reluctance came over him and he asked to be sent away, 'far out of sight of this town'. This, of course, is extremely odd; the slave certainly lost no time on the way, yet when he comes to Thebes he finds Oedipus already installed. Sophocles indulges here in a slight foreshortening. This memory of Jocasta's is quite impossible—the thing she recalls could not have occurred; on the other hand it is very good drama. This strange behaviour of the herdsman makes a notable piece in the pattern. Things are beginning to slip into place for Jocasta: she is deeply uneasy now.[1]

Or take the management of the agents and envoys. If all this had been happening in life, about four of these would have been needed. There would have been the man who escaped from the cross-roads; there would have been the man who took away the child; there would have been the man who received the child; and there would have been the man who brought the message from Corinth. Sophocles reduces them to two, by identifying the first with the second, and identifying the third with the fourth.

We concede this move easily enough; and do those sundry 'punctualities' cause us much deeper distress? Dr Norwood thinks that some of them do. In a sense, the two shepherds just mentioned hold the fate of Oedipus in their hands; their paths must converge at Thebes—they must arrive within the same hour—to precipitate the full disclosure. Each holds half of the riddle, and if one or other had been absent the whole truth need not have emerged. (There is a pretty case here of what may be described as dramatic supercession. The old Theban was, of course, originally summoned to pronounce on the circumstances of the slaying; but by the time he arrives on the scene the importance of this has faded into the background; the vital issue now is: who gave him the infant to expose?) That the Corinthian messenger should arrive so pat is, of course, the sheerest coincidence, and I doubt whether we do the play a service by trying to smooth it over. Dr Norwood, to save the day, suggests that we might consider whether coincidence itself is not natural; life,

[1] See J. T. Sheppard, *op. cit.*, p. 148.

after all, does include accidents; so that, in a sense, all that Sophocles is doing is 'mirroring the facts' of life; and perhaps this was his very intention. I would suggest that it is utterly obvious that Sophocles had no such idea in his mind. Life here is far from his thoughts; he is merely trying for a neat construction. He knows that he is being a little incredible but he can count on us (he feels) to co-operate. Again, it is a mutual pact; we allow him the leeway he requires and refrain from vexatious objections; he, on his part, tightens his plot and saves us many moments of dullness.

Or consider, for a final instance, the disclosure by Oedipus of his birth. 'My father was Polybus of Corinth, my mother the Dorian Merope.' He makes this announcement to the Queen, and proceeds to tell her why it was he left Corinth. So he has never mentioned the matter before: what an unconcerned pair they have been! We can say, with Mr Sheppard, that it is merely the 'grand manner' again. That may be a part of the truth; the touch of formality in such utterances certainly makes their reception the easier.[1] But in this case it is surely not the whole of the truth. The technique is essentially transparent: Oedipus relates these things to Jocasta because somehow they must be told. Mr Sheppard comments on the passage: 'Of course Jocasta knows that he is supposed to be the son of Polybus.'[2] I do not think that this is strictly true. It might be true if we were dealing with history, but because we are dealing with a drama the truth is slightly different. The question of Jocasta's knowledge or ignorance does not really enter the drama; it

---

[1] Cf. vv. 1042-3: '*Messenger*. I think he was called one of the household of Laius. *Oedipus*. The king who ruled this country long ago?' This seems purely formality.　　　　　　　　　　　　　　　　[2] *Op. cit.*, p. 148.

is left, so to speak, a blur; Sophocles deliberately smudges that point. What Mr Sheppard does in his comment is to attempt to re-draw that smudge; but Sophocles does not wish it re-drawn. The matter at issue here may be trifling, but the principle behind it is vital; when dramatists blur some detail it is because they desire it blurred; when they take pains not to raise a question then that question is *not in the play*.

What, then, is to be our verdict on this drama? What shall we say of this close-knit web of ironies that constitutes the *Oedipus Tyrannus*?

The chief problems that I have discussed resolve themselves largely, it may be, into questions of emphasis; but these are of the utmost importance. The character of Oedipus is not itself in dispute; the question is of the emphasis that this character has received in the play. I do not think for my own part that the portrayal of Oedipus is a masterpiece; it seems to me rather absurd to suggest that he is the 'best-drawn character in Sophocles'.[1] I doubt whether we ever *feel* his nature quite as we feel the nature of Antigone—or, indeed, as we feel the nature of the aged Oedipus himself. We recognize that he has this or that quality, but do we ever quite reach the core? And his qualities have to some extent to adapt themselves to the exigencies of the plot. There is not a perfect coherence between that sagacious Oedipus of the past and this present unpredictable Oedipus whose brain seems so often befogged and who is swayed so easily by his passions. Oedipus is an assembly of qualities; they are a little loosely collected, and

[1] Gilbert Norwood, *op. cit.*, p. 149.

there is no clear *soul* in the man that makes qualities largely irrelevant; unless we are content just to speak of nobility. He becomes clearer to us after his downfall; we begin then really to see him, and perceive that his structure is truly heroic. But his character is not the point of the play.

It is the same with the different 'theses' that have been seen as underlying the drama. We know little of Sophocles' religion. When we sum up what we know of his beliefs we find them meagre in number and depressingly commonplace in quality. He thought it was best to commit no injustice and, on the whole, to avoid excess. He believed that there are ups and downs in fortunes, and that men are never secure. (An account of Shakespeare's religion would produce somewhat similar results.) There is religion in the *Oedipus Tyrannus* but it is not all crucial in the drama. Mr Webster holds the opinion that Sophocles set great store by oracles. It may well be, of course, that he did. But I would suggest that there is a simple reason for the frequency of oracles in his plays: they are excellent story-material. And as for the oracles here, it is surely quite preposterous to say that 'Sophocles wrote the *Tyrannus* to defend what was for him, as for Socrates, one of the basic facts of religion'.[1]

He did not write it for that, nor did he write it in a laborious attempt to prove that the gods like giving men lessons; nor did he write it in order to explain. After all, how could he explain? Oedipus is indisputably a victim; that fact is at the very heart of the drama. 'O Zeus, what hast thou willed to do unto me?'—this is the central cry of the play. A thorough thinking through of the facts could have led only to an indictment of the gods. Sophocles draws

[1] T. B. L. Webster, *op. cit.*, p. 23.

back from such an indictment. But this is merely an abstinence, and does not bestow 'meaning' on the drama. There is no meaning in the *Oedipus Tyrannus*. There is merely the terror of coincidence, and then, at the end of it all, our impression of man's power to suffer, and of his greatness because of this power.

The theme is not, then, universal. The theme of *Lear* is universal; but what the *Oedipus Tyrannus* rests on is a frightful groundwork of accident. Its driving forces are not feelings (though the object of nearly all criticism of the play is to prove, by desperate measures, that they are). There is feeling enough in the play, but other forces than feeling produce it. It is best to take it as it is. It is so great in its kind that we hurt it in trying to help it.

How did its special qualities arise? As I suggest, we may perhaps observe in Greek drama an especial responsiveness to themes; it moulds itself to its themes, reflects their merits and defects, with a somewhat exceptional readiness. We have here a most unusual theme, a theme superbly suited to all that Greek drama could do best. It works through a passive situation; but the passive situation, because of the peculiar nature of this case, becomes instinct with dramatic life. Hardly anything happens, beyond people arriving with news. We watch how the pieces of a puzzle fall one by one into place. Yet can one think of a drama so vibrant with the sense of event?

We needed four or five of the other six tragedies to take the full measure of Sophocles, but, as dramatist, he is here at his bourn. This is the unapproachable play.

CHAPTER IX

DOOM OR TRIUMPH? THE *ELECTRA*

A CONNOISSEUR in the vagaries of dramatic criticism would be hard put to it, even by search, to discover a happier hunting-ground than in recent comment on the Sophoclean *Electra*. The case is particularly neat and satisfying because to the unprejudiced eye (and I may as well make my assertions defiantly) there is simply no problem at all. Cloudy places exist in Sophocles; there are difficulties that, after all our thought, we must leave; but difficulties of that kind are not here. Indeed it would not be easy to think of a play that more manifestly and unmistakably fulfils its limited intention. The incrustations of recent criticism have come about from one sole cause—from a refusal to admit that the intentions of the drama were limited. The result is a really beautiful 'problem', a problem that would have much astonished the dramatist, and that fades into nothingness at once if we merely remind ourselves of how a drama is constituted, of the restrictions within which it works, of what it can and cannot do. The case is not like that of (say) *Hamlet*, where, make what efforts we will, we still feel at the end an uncertainty, for in that play there are suggestions of meanings not fully worked out in the action, and whether these meanings are really there, or whether they are, in the main, our illusion— this we have no hope of knowing, for there would be only one way to know and that would be to get Shakespeare and ask him. The *Electra* is not at all like this. There is no aura of unclarified meanings, of ideas not successfully embodied. Sophocles embodied everything he wished to. The problem of this play arises because it is sometimes felt that he should have embodied more. But if we merely cling tight to the fact that Sophocles here, as everywhere, was a dramatist with a dramatist's preoccupations, all difficulties disappear. We may say, I think, with perfect assurance, that the case is thus and thus; that such and such judgments about the play are errors, that such and such judgments are true. Perhaps nowhere else in Sophocles is an equal downrightness possible.

Let us review the play by stages, taking in turn the critical questions that arise.

The first seventy-six verses set the scene. They perform the all-important office of *stationing* us, of giving us a certain angle of vision. (Opening passages in this way are always crucial. They set our faces in a certain direction, impose an orientation hard to break.) The lines also give us a rapid prospect of events that will presently unroll. Orestes, with the Paedagogus and Pylades, has just arrived at Argos: stands drinking in the scene. The task, so long planned for, is at hand. The old man says they must take final counsels, go over their project once again. Orestes, accordingly, for the benefit of the audience, recapitulates the decisions he has made—decisions, of course, that his two friends must by now know very well at heart. He consulted the Pythian oracle to learn how best to proceed, and was strongly advised by Phoebus to make it a private adventure—not to rally a force of helpers but to put his trust in secrecy and stealth; hence their little band of three. The old man is first to make a reconnaissance; he is to watch his opportunity and slip inside the palace, partly to report on conditions and partly to spread the news that Orestes has perished at the games. The two young men, in the meanwhile, will repair to the tomb of Agamemnon in order to crown it with appropriate offerings, and will pick up on their way back the urn with Orestes' 'ashes'. So, often, says Orestes, the rumour of death has been the prelude to intenser living. He hopes that he too, by this ruse, shall go on to win renown, and that he may enjoy the assistance of the gods in restoring his father's house. On this note the little group breaks up and its members leave on their several missions.

I do not think that for an unprejudiced spectator there could be two opinions about the meaning of this scene. It is preliminary, but it is of the utmost importance. Later on there may be surprises (we do not know at this moment) but a good dramatist will never wilfully mislead us by the tones of his opening sequence. They are as important in announcing and foretelling as the opening bars of a symphony. What they tell us, in this case, is unmistakable. What is said is as clear as day, and that which is *not* said is just as significant. There is simply no missing the cues. Take, for example, the question of the oracle (the truth is, of course, that there is no question). It does not help our understanding of the passage—on the contrary, it very gravely impairs it —to amass from history and legend (as Mr Sheppard and others have done) evidence bearing on the falsity of oracles. There are many and many accounts of men who sought the advice of oracles and came to grief for their pain. Generally it was their own fault. They approached the oracle insincerely, they kept back an element of the truth, they wished to obtain a warrant for some nefarious procedure; and they found the oracle too clever for them. It is plain, then, that oracles are dangerous; their utterances can be very deceptive and they are not to be lightly invoked. All this we readily grant; but it makes not one particle of difference to the opening scene of this play. Historical research here is wasted; it merely blurs what was crystal-clear. Not *every* oracle is malicious, and though men have been grievously misled, oracles still do not exist to mislead. They have their use and authority, their function in the scheme of things. The point is that no dramatist could take for granted that his audience would consider every oracle deceptive; he could not possibly afford to leave it to his audience to make up their minds about an oracle. It is true that Orestes has put a leading question, and that oracles seem irritated by leading questions as a rule. It is true also that the advice this oracle did give is somewhat lacking in pregnancy: we may imagine that Orestes' unaided intelligence could have brought him somewhere near that conclusion—namely, that the best way to go about this particular project was by stealth and sudden assault. But these are irrelevant matters. We have to judge of this oracle by our impressions, and to some extent by what is understood in the story: and on neither count is there room for a doubt. Apollo may not expressly have commanded the murder, but he says enough to imply quite certainly that what Orestes is about has his full approval. It is putting it far too mildly to say that any other view is 'hazardous'.[1] Any other view is in flat contradiction to the definite sense of the drama. If there had been the slightest

[1] H. D. F. Kitto, *op. cit.*, p. 131.

question about Apollo's attitude, Sophocles would have been bound, as a dramatist, to raise it.

Let us stay for a moment longer on this prelude. Of all critics Mr Sheppard has perhaps been the most vigorous in condemning the young Orestes. He sees him as impulsive, but 'not overscrupulous', going to Delphi with his mind made up and asking ambiguously, impiously, 'By what means can I take vengeance on the murderers?' And, as Mr Sheppard sees it, he receives his reward. The god 'replies according to the questioner's folly'—deceiving the would-be deceiver—and Orestes rushes break-neck to destruction.[1] As I say, such a picture seems to me to negate the clear impression of the play; and so does a minor picture with which Mr Sheppard supplements this main one. It is of the Paedagogus as the arch-corrupter, the perverter of the young man's mind. In the opening speech the Paedagogus recalls how he carried Orestes into safety and reared him up to manhood, to avenge the slaughter of his sire. 'So the poet tells us with what skill the youth's affections have been all his life exploited for the purpose of the vengeance.'[2] Mr Kitto is one who has found this view sympathetic. I would suggest that it has no basis whatever but is clean contrary to what Sophocles intends. The Paedagogus trained Orestes and kept in mind his ultimate mission: but 'exploit' is totally unjustified. Such a word can only derive from one's own moral view of the vengeance. If we discovered as the action proceeded that this was also the view of the drama the situation of course would be altered. I suggest strongly that we cannot discover it. But as far as this first scene is concerned no slightest overtone exists that could imply that

[1] *Classical Review*, XLI (1927), p. 4.   [2] *Ibid.*

Orestes was 'exploited'. The first scene, as I say, gives us our bearings; its importance in that way in incalculable. To undo what was done in that scene would be a nearly impossible task for a dramatist—its marks are virtually ineffaceable; and it places us firmly and securely on the side of Orestes and his friends. The impression of the first scene is this. The little party of three is on the brink of a grim adventure; it is to be grim, by its very nature, and there will be problems of ways and means; but no other kind of worry afflicts them. There is no faintest sign of a conflict—of a conflict now or to come. Their minds are smooth of all trouble: there are no doubts, no hesitations, no qualms. Their decisions have been long ago taken; they seem to feel their duty as beyond question. In short, their frame of mind is highly efficient: they have no care in the world beyond the practical problems ahead.[1] At this stage we do not know what is in store for us. It is possible that a sudden change may come. Orestes may not have judged his own nature as accurately as perhaps he has imagined (there is, of course, no sign in the drama that he has been guilty of any introspection at all). But he could go to pieces at a pinch when he sees what the vengeance implies. All this is in the lap of the drama. Our business is very simple: it is simply to wait and see. Whatever emerges will concern us, but our concern will be only with what emerges. At this point we can say unhesitatingly: the horizon is free of all clouds.

The next phase is again clearly defined: it begins with the entrance of Electra. There are two comments, I think, to make about this sequence, which takes us to v. 515.

---

[1] 'A mixture of matricide and good spirits': this paraphrase of Schlegel's description really hits off the play rather well.

In the first place, it is not even yet suggested that we are in the presence of emotional conflicts. Electra's state is wretched, but the quality of her wretchedness is noteworthy. She is obviously an exceptional person. We see her first in contrast with the Chorus. The Chorus, representing normality—representing, that is to say, the humdrum, everyday outlook, moving on the level of proverbial maxims, typifying ordinary homespun morality—vent the criticisms that we naturally expect from them. They say: 'Why make your life miserable? What have you to gain from it all? Why struggle against the inevitable? Why spoil your whole life attempting to remedy what is done with and past all cure?' All the instincts of the Chorus are for compromise: they advise her to adapt herself, be sensible, come to terms. They admit that the deed was heinous and that the guilty ones really ought to be punished, and they try to instil into her the comforting thought that perhaps in fullness of time they will be. In the meantime, what can she do? Electra sees the force of their arguments; on any realistic view her chance of success is negligible. Her difficulty consists in the simple fact that she is unable to change her nature. Right and wrong are so real to her that the sight of a scandalous maladjustment between the two affects her like a physical agony. She is prepared to suspend the whole business of living while she tries to correct the injustice. We observe her with amazement, thinking: 'Perhaps life ought to be lived on this level; perhaps this is how the whole process of living would look if moral principles were the realities they should be'; and then we recoil from the picture of a world frequented by Electras. She has already made the guilty pay—their life lately has been no bed of roses. 'I harry them', she says. She has resisted all their overtures, her one aim has been to be a thorn in their sides. She pours scorn on Chrysothemis the collaborator, who has reached a *modus vivendi* with the murderers and now has ease and plenteous living. Electra, in short, is the very image of righteous recalcitrance, and possesses, as well, a moral fastidiousness that makes her shudder, as at a lapse of taste, when she is told of Clytaemnestra's tributes for the tomb. These feelings of moral fitness are the deep well-springs of her conduct.

But let us not read more into her conduct than is there. Her friends, understandably, think her odd, but we, who are privileged to see more deeply, are not entitled to count her 'queer'. She possesses an amazing integrity, her moral stamina is exceptional, she is also unusually ruthless, and she is endowed with a quite remarkable power of persisting in any course she has chosen. Her behaviour may seem eccentric, but the motives behind it are natural. Above all, she has no conflicts. In the sequence that we are at present considering there is no suggestion anywhere that she doubted herself for a moment. There is no tug of contraries within her. She knows, of course, how she must appear to others, and her long speech at v. 254 is an appeal for comprehension. She must seem froward, irreverent, unreasonable; but how can one in her circumstances be a model of perfect behaviour? 'In such a case, then, friends, there is no room for moderation or for reverence.'[1] She asserts the validity of excess. A quite exceptional duty has fallen to her and only an extremist can solve it. But she is not, herself, aghast at the task nor is her nature disrupted. Her inmost self is as much at peace as Orestes'; she, too, is an efficient engine for her mission. As

[1] Vv. 307-8.

she spits out her hate of the murderers—'May the great god of Olympus send them their dues of suffering!'[1]—we feel how fiercely all her forces are marshalled, how tense and unclouded is her vision.

This leads to a second consideration. I have insisted more than once or twice in these pages on the paramount importance of the 'natural response'. This is automatic with an ordinary reader, but with a student it can be thrown out of gear. Just as a compass on ship or aircraft is subject to various kinds of interference, so with a scholar many things conspire to throw his natural response out of alignment. It is like a delicate, indispensable instrument that has to be continually watched and overhauled periodically for correction. For nothing is easier, in the study, than to brood too closely over a play; and in the course of such intensive brooding perspectives can become a little distorted—indeed the distortion can become immense. Features start out from the play that had no real existence within it; the whole *relief* of a play can be changed, its whole lighting and shading upset.

All this has a most definite bearing on matricide in the *Electra*. I suppose there was never a spectator—and there could not very well have been a reader—who was not clearly aware from the beginning that this play would include two murders. Aegisthus is doomed to be killed, and so, as certainly, is Clytaemnestra. Matricide is in the scheme of the play from the outset; and Mr Sheppard is right when he declares that even in the sequences that we are at present considering there are clear hints of what is to come. And even if nothing had been mentioned, it stands to reason that

[1] Vv. 209-10.

thoughts of both killings would have been constantly in the mind of Electra. But here comes the risk of error—of losing sight of the *relief* of a drama. By very careful lighting and shading it is possible to give even matricide an extraordinary range of values in a drama. The effect of it can be diminished to a degree that one would not have thought possible. Precisely this is what Sophocles is about; and it is interesting to see how he does it. For one thing, he never stays longer than he can help on the subject. He does not give the appearance of avoiding it (for that would have been equally a mistake) but he is most careful never to dwell on it.[1] He makes Electra use phrases of this kind whenever she draws near to the subject: she speaks of the murder done 'by my mother and her bedfellow Aegisthus' (97-8); she prays that Zeus will requite them with suffering (209-10); she fears an end of all decency and right-living if a dead man is just to lie in the dust while his slayers go on as before (244-50); she trusts that Orestes may still be alive somewhere and that one day he will trample on his enemies (455-56). Of course such phrases imply that Clytaemnestra is marked down for killing; but do they excite in us a feeling of the horror? On the contrary, they are purposely edgeless, they have almost no emotional bite. These hints are not really sinister; they hardly graze the mind in passing and add nothing to what we knew before. Nothing is clearer than that by all these tactics Sophocles is neutralizing the effect of the matricide. Indeed his caution is such that he

---

[1] See A. S. Owen in the *Classical Review*, XLI (1927), pp. 50-2. Mr Owen is admirable on this point. I do not agree with him in his conception of the 'tragedy' of Electra. I think he concedes far too much in the second half of his valuable note.

reaches the verge of absurdity, for it would be unnatural if from time to time there were not some suggestion of what Electra must be thinking. He stops just this side of the unnaturalness: he gives us just enough to prevent us from inquiring, yet so little that the idea of the matricide is drained of its horrifying force. Mr Sheppard says: 'It is not true that in the structure of this play the shadow of the coming matricide is negligible.'[1] But I think that that is precisely what is true: it is for that very result that Sophocles is working. He cannot hurl the matricide from his play, for it is part and parcel of his subject, but he can choose his own way of treating it; and the way that he has chosen is to deprive it of imaginative value. At least, that is his technique up to this point (and I think it is his technique to the end). In these first five hundred lines of the play, though matricide is of course a postulate, the thought of it is not allowed to become real. Every reference is carefully colourless. Words play vaguely about it—fall, so to speak, on either side of it; not one word strikes home. We arrive, that is to say, once more at the contrast between a drama and a document. If the *Electra* were a transcript of reality then we might peer into it as closely as we pleased: there would be no danger of upsetting proportions, of losing sight of carefully arranged perspectives. But a drama is, in fact, an arrangement; if we destroy this, all goes down.

Let us apply the same principle to the next sequence, which is the colloquy between mother and daughter. Again, I do not think that an unprejudiced reader can have two opinions about the drift. We have already been compelled to take sides. (This is something that we cannot help: it is no use

---

[1] *Classical Review*, XLI (1927), p. 164.

our struggling against it. Give a drama five minutes to work on us and it can align us with this side or that; our sympathies are in its control.) The *Electra* has been in progress many minutes by the time Clytaemnestra appears (in fact, a third of the play is now over) and everything that we have so far heard has been extremely damaging to her cause. This, indeed, is putting it far too mildly. Our attitude to her by now is such that it would take a revolution to overthrow it. She is a cruel and cowardly murderess who lacks even a streak of audacity to win our reluctant respect. She is not an imposing criminal, like Goneril; her affinities are rather with Regan. She leans by nature to treachery; when safe, she is spiteful and impudent. She is a woman lost to all decencies, who will stoop to any degradation to make her position secure. Then this woman and Electra meet. We *cannot* listen to their debate cold-bloodedly, because we have already been influenced by the play. It is not as if we are waiting to hear who is right—we know that before they begin. In other words, if Sophocles had really intended in this scene to show that Electra's case was imperfect—if he had really wished us to see that what she was planning was bad, and that she was plunging on towards a gulf—then he would have needed to make tremendous exertions to overcome the sympathies and antipathies already planted. Innuendos would not have sufficed. It would never have done to have sown stray hints, and to have left us to ferret them out. He would have had to make his meaning unmistakable.

Of course he has done nothing of the kind. It is true that Electra's speech is not logical. That is to say, if we reflect on it and analyse it fairly closely we can see that the reasoning is flawed and that there is a basic inconsistency underlying it; and about the speech as a whole we may have the feeling that we could ourselves, with some little thought, have improved on it. If this task had fallen to us, of meeting Clytaemnestra's arguments with arguments, and of marshalling all our facts for one final annihilating rejoinder, we may feel that we could have done better. There were many speeches that Sophocles could have written for Electra, and no amount of pondering will ever help us to know why he wrote this one and not another. It is possible that he felt the task, in essence, so easy that he did not take immoderate pains—that he was so assured that we would be with Electra that he merely did not trouble to make her case stronger; and in that opinion he was perfectly right. Electra's onslaught is more than adequate for its purpose; it sweeps her opponent from the field.

She comes to the heart of the matter at once: 'You say yourself that you killed my father.' Now in logic (as Mr Kitto says) every further step she takes from this point renders her own position the less tenable. If even punitive slaying is bad, what of the deed she herself intends? It is no matter—this is a trifling problem for a dramatist. A drama can absorb such an inconsistency without a trace of strain or effort. The illogicalities that matter in a drama are the illogicalities that are brought into focus—not the illogicalities that are buried. This illogicality of Electra's is buried. We do not notice it as we read, or if we do its effect is negligible. It is only brought into focus when we meditate over the play, and especially when we reinspect the play in the light of some theory we may cherish.

And exactly the same comment applies to her account of

the original offence. She delves into the mythological background:

Ask the huntress Artemis what sin she punished when she stayed the frequent winds at Aulis; or I will tell thee; for we may not learn from her. My father—so I have heard—was once disporting himself in the grove of the goddess, when his footfall startled a dappled and antlered stag; he shot it, and chanced to utter a certain boast concerning its slaughter. Wroth thereat the daughter of Leto detained the Greeks, that, in quittance for the wild creature's life, my father should yield up the life of his own child. Thus it befell that she was sacrificed; since the fleet had no other release, homeward or to Troy; and for that cause, under sore constraint and with sore reluctance, at last he slew her—not for the sake of Menelaus.[1]

This is one of those parts of her rejoinder that (if we had been uttering it) we feel we might have improved on. The introduction of the legend is a little awkward; and perhaps, tactically, she might have done better. Nevertheless it is a reply, and it effectively clears Agamemnon. The passage may be somewhat laboured and frigid, but these defects would need to be ten times as obtrusive if they were to tell us that Electra was faltering. 'Her boldness and assurance leave her . . . she produces this unreal excuse for Agamemnon in a moment, one might almost say, of panic.'[2] This is what Mr Kitto deduces from the speech. Surely such deductions are out of the question; that is weighting the passage with a meaning that it cannot even begin to sustain.

She returns then to the direct attack, and there is no awkwardness in anything that follows. She exposes Clytaemnestra's real motive—infatuation with Aegisthus; she charges her with shameless conduct—living openly with a

[1] Vv. 563-76, trans. Jebb. [2] H. D. F. Kitto, *op. cit.*, p. 133.

murderer and casting out Agamemnon's children; she asks, neatly, if this also is justice—vengeance for a daughter's blow; and then she loses her patience. What are reasonings to Clytaemnestra who merely shrieks in rejoinder that a daughter is insulting a mother. 'Mother! taskmistress rather.' Electra leaves her virtually in tears.

The vileness of Clytaemnestra is pointed markedly by the scene that immediately ensues. She is the epitome of meanness and cowardly caution as she dispatches her maid to the tomb—the very type of those who would be pardoned and yet would retain the offence. She is almost comical in her prayer to Apollo—the brazenness of it is sublime. She puts all the responsibility on him; first he must interpret her dream, then act according to its meaning. If it bodes well for her, fulfil it; if ill, let her enemies suffer. She gives Apollo as it were a wink to take note of what she has left unexpressed; he cannot go wrong (so she adjures him) if he looks beneath her words and simply gives her what her heart desires. If ever a prayer deserved to misfire this indecent petition did, and it gets its punctual reward, for hard upon it, almost as its answer, comes the entry of the aged servant with his story of Orestes' death. Clytaemnestra drops a tear—and notes her emotion with surprise. It is only a passing pang, a reaction of some nerve of motherhood, not quite atrophied even in her. She smothers it with no trouble. The feeling that floods her being is one of vast relief.

The *tour de force* of the Paedagogus calls merely for our tribute in passing, but upon its back, as it were, a curious question of interpretation has arisen. It is extremely odd that it should ever have been suggested that we are taken in by this speech. Kaibel, it seems, first made this suggestion; it received the favour then, strangely enough, of the shrewd Wilamowitz;[1] since then Mr T. B. L. Webster has adopted it. It is surely the oddest of notions. What it does is to turn an Athenian audience into a collection of Partridges at the Play; indeed one wonders whether Partridge himself could have compassed this measure of naïveté. It is to be remembered that we have been told all the facts and that we have seen Orestes alive. Of course, the speech carries us away; that is to say, we respond imaginatively to its pictures. But it is a mere commonplace of dramatic experience that we can do all this very well and yet know that the facts are otherwise. Imaginative sympathy is one thing, conviction of truth another. The general principle is exceedingly clear; and the situation in the *Electra* so obvious that it would not warrant a moment's discussion if (for reasons very difficult to penetrate) the scholars mentioned had not brought up the issue.

Electra, even after hearing the dire tale of the Paedagogus, is still not utterly defeated, and makes an effort to enlist the help of Chrysothemis.

There is one point, I think, of great importance in this scene. Its positive meanings are clear, but in what happens there is also a negative meaning of the highest significance

---

[1] For, whatever one thinks of the general approach of this scholar, this is not the kind of aberration one would have expected of him; nor can I quite convince myself that he has full faith in what he says. He maintains that even today a spectator would be so worked upon by the speech that he would become quite oblivious of the facts in the background, and that this is what Sophocles intended. Sophocles put forth all his craft 'um uns trotz unseres besseren Wissens zu zwingen, die Lügenbotschaft für wahr zu halten' (*Die Dramatische Technik des Sophokles* [1917], p. 191).

for the drift of the play. Electra makes her overture to Chrysothemis; it is a clever, diplomatic appeal. We may imagine that, as she comes to the point, she watches the face of Chrysothemis somewhat nervously. She names only one name—Aegisthus; it would have been out of the question to risk more.[1] Then she persuasively sets out the case. As things are, what future is there even for Chrysothemis? Aegisthus will never let her wed. There is little, then, to be lost by action while much may conceivably be gained; freedom, happiness, glory, and no doubt a successful marriage as well. The world will acclaim the sisters who dared to strike a blow for justice—who put their lives in jeopardy to retrieve the honour of their house. Electra presses and pleads, tries all approaches that she thinks might be of avail.

She does not succeed with her sister, but the replies of Chrysothemis are noteworthy. If (as Mr Sheppard and Mr Kitto believe) matricide is already entrenched in the play, why is it that Chrysothemis does not seize at once on this horror? Mr Sheppard speaks of the tell-tale plurals; we have one of those plurals here (979); but it has no effect on Chrysothemis; she resorts to quite other objections. Kindly and well-intentioned, but with no spark of her sister's greatness, with nothing of the inspiration that lifts Electra to these exceptional levels, she is merely repelled and frightened. Her reasonings are customary and conventional: they are

---

[1] 'She is now deceiving herself as well as Chrysothemis . . . she refuses to think of the worse part of what lies before her' (G. M. Kirkwood, 'Two Structural Features of Sophocles' *Electra*', *Transactions and Proceedings of the American Philological Association*, LXXIII [1942], p. 90). It is quite illegitimate to draw this inference at the time, and it would be legitimate to draw it afterwards only if it were strongly reinforced by later impressions. There is not a particle of such reinforcement.

women (what can women do against men?); the whole scheme is madness itself. But it will be observed that she does not say what one would have expected her to say—that the scheme is a horror of impiety. Her abstention is, in reality, unnatural; for who would have been more likely than Chrysothemis to read what was in the mind of Electra? Her timidity would have made her acute. Her regard for the accepted standards would have made her especially alert. In real life she could hardly have helped divining what Electra's suggestions implied. She is made preternaturally dense, and this is for an ulterior purpose. It is to further the designs of Sophocles, who is still keeping the matricide repressed—still keeping that motif subdued, still cushioning our minds against the shudder of what that second killing will imply.

I would insist again on the point, for it seems to me utterly crucial. If Mr Sheppard and Mr Kitto were right, then it seems to me absolutely certain that this scene would not be as it is. Sophocles would have been a veritable bungler to have toned down the matricide here. Here was his grand opportunity to bring it fully home to our feelings. If he had been thinking of a tragedy of Electra, here was his great chance to establish it. But to me it is abundantly clear that what we have been watching in these scenes has been something very different from the unrolling of tragedy. There are slayings, of course, to come, but no tragedy is to be involved for the slayers. What we have been watching has been an exhibition, by a master, of the *art of dramatic suppression*. That is the dominant technique of this play. How a horror can be sapped of its strength, how a crime can be so drained of its power to shock that we are left in full sympathy with the criminals, how an offence against nature can be smothered and we can be led to accept an atrocity—this is the technical lesson of the *Electra*.

Let us come to the final sequences. The recognition scene, beautifully handled as it is, calls for no particular comment. The change in Electra is instantaneous. This is a surge in her of joy and confidence; obstacles that seemed so formidable become trifles scarcely worth a thought. Her new mood makes Orestes anxious; he counsels caution, restraint. But Electra is above all fears—'those womenfolk in the house, stay-at-homes, superfluities, dead weights upon the earth'— why fear danger from such as they? Orestes still tries to repress her, but her exhilaration is beyond checking. Her feeling now is that destiny is with them and that nothing will or can go wrong. She feels too that her recovery of Orestes has an almost symbolic import; it works upon her strangely, she says; if Agamemnon himself were to appear she would be ready to believe him real. I would suggest that in our imaginative experience of this play nothing is more important than to take in to the fullest these impressions—to yield ourselves without reserve to this tide of feeling in Electra. Will it not be conceded that for a tragic figure she is now moving with considerable freedom— showing, as the critical moments draw near, a remarkable buoyancy of spirit, an amazing self-confidence and ease?

And really, if we continue to yield to the drama, we can hardly be in doubt for a moment as to the significance of all that is happening. The Paedagogus calls them sharply to action; no time now for talk and rejoicings; and from now on what the drama presents is simply the working out of the high, grim enterprise. As Orestes and Pylades enter the palace Electra prays for the success of their venture: 'O

Lycean Apollo, I beg, I implore, I beseech, give kindly aid to us in those things we plan, and show to men what recompense the gods bestow on the wicked.' Hers are the accents of authentic prayer as contrasted with Clytaemnestra's humbug. We resist the effect of this passage only at the cost of distorting the drama. Electra is fierce, it is true. There is something terrible in the sight of her cheering on the murderers from a distance. She listens till the sounds begin, then re-enacts each stage of the drama. She clenches her teeth in sympathy, imitates the striking of the blows: 'Strike, if thou canst, again!'; it is one of the terrible cries of the play. She has a running patter of savage repartee for the shrieks and pleadings from indoors. She coaches the slayers in their task, watches the situation as it develops. She enjoys her ironies with Aegisthus, sees when the moment has come to gag him ('Brother, in the name of heaven, let there be a stop put now to his talking, do not allow him to start making speeches'). But in these feverish moments is she tragic? Only if we presume to apply our own version of what such conduct ought to entail. There can be no tragedy in a work of fiction if the character concerned does not feel it. Electra ought, perhaps, to be riven with conflicts, but that does not give us the right to conclude that she is. It is obvious that in this scene she is in her element; she feels it her 'finest hour'; she was never so happy as at this moment. We may be very grieved by these facts and be extremely sorry for Electra. But how if she is not sorry for herself? Then we are merely beating the air.

But, indeed, there is not the lightest question about the point of view of the play. The Chorus are wholeheartedly with the killers; not once in these later furious scenes have they even suggested a qualm. And who else has shown hesitation, has drawn even momentarily back? Electra asks Orestes how he fared. 'All's well within', he says, 'if well Apollo spake.' It is futile to dig for a meaning. Do the words indicate a possible reaction? Is Orestes feeling a twinge of remorse? Has he at last a vague doubt of the oracle? We could accept it as a natural touch if Orestes were showing a slight sinking of the spirit; so doubtful is the interpretation of his words that we can have no assurance that he is. But if he were, it would be of little consequence. His recovery is extraordinarily rapid, and, as far as we can tell, complete. The weakness—if it ever existed—has a negligible effect on the drama. In itself it is so transient and doubtful, and other impressions so choke it, that it amounts to a veritable nothing. As for carrying his reaction forward and associating it with that pause while he bandies words with Aegisthus—this, surely, is to lapse into fancies. 'Orestes has discovered that the death of his mother is an appalling thing. It has shaken him far more than he foresaw. He has no rational qualms about killing Aegisthus, but he shrinks from it and has to be kept to it.'[1] This is sheer reconstruction. Mr Bowra is not here interpreting the play, he is indulging himself with rewriting it.

So with the concluding words. A dramatist simply cannot spring ironies on us in the last ten lines of his play. No cues are possible then. The play is over, for better or worse; the dramatist has conveyed his meaning or he has not. When Orestes, half turning to the audience, says, 'See how the lawless die', we are not meant to detect hidden satire on the recent course of events; and when the Chorus make their

[1] C. M. Bowra, *op. cit.*, p. 253.

habitual pronouncement and add the final flourish to the drama, we are intended (if we listen at all) to believe simply and fully what they say. The agonies of this family are over. The House of Atreus has been tried as by fire, but now clear days stretch ahead: that is what the parting words of the Chorus mean, and that is all that they mean.

But we can fill in the picture a little from hints that we have already received. What does the future hold for Orestes and Electra? I insist again that it is not our business to argue this matter theoretically. Perhaps there *ought* to have been bleak days ahead. Can they really settle down happily after the experiences they have just lived through? Will they not pay for them sooner or later? Will there not be delayed effects, in nervous sufferings and exhaustions? In real life there would have been some such consequences; dramatically, we know nothing about them. The drama is cut off short— the theme, in this sense, is truncated. All those possibilities are ignored, the fact being that Sophocles deliberately refrains from probing. For all that we know, dramatically, brother and sister lived happily ever after. More—this is the definite implication of the drama. The play does not even end with a question-mark. 'When we're successful, there'll be time for gladness and rejoicing in freedom.'[1] Such sayings are all-important for the tone. So we hear that the ancient curse is fading. The Paedagogus looks forward to the day when the friends shall exchange reminiscences—just now the moment is too urgent, there is no leisure for retailing the past. We may not note these items in passing, but they affect our emotional response: they create the *atmosphere* of the ending. And what word can apply to it but 'happy'? Not only are

[1] Vv. 1299-1300.

the Erinyes not lurking; they are not on the visible horizon. As far as this play is concerned, they are never to enter the story.

I add two or three notes in conclusion.

There are echoes of Aeschylus in the *Electra*, but I think we should beware of taking this fact too seriously or of deducing from it a critical principle. In the upshot, nothing can relieve a dramatist from the responsibility for his own plays. Further, we can exaggerate the need for comparisons when two dramas happen to share a theme. We have little trouble in this respect today, and it is unlikely that Athenian audiences had more. A good drama is self-contained, and audiences are not hard put to it as a rule to keep one drama distinct from another. We can see at a glance that Athenian audiences had no trouble of that sort with characters; they were not confused by the different versions of Odysseus, they held their Creons separate in the mind. When we read M. Sartre's *Les Mouches*, do we find our memories intruding, or even mingling in any appreciable degree with these new impressions of Orestes and Electra? We take M. Sartre's points the more keenly because they are so original and so strange. But it would be just as absurd to say that we can only read M. Sartre with profit when we have our Aeschylus and our Sophocles beside us. In short, when Professor George Thomson declares that we can only really understand a play of Sophocles when we have the Aeschylean version for comparison (in those cases where the subjects were identical) I think we may fairly rebel. The Aeschylean *Oedipus* is missing—so our appreciation of the other is imperfect. This is surely an impossible attitude. It would be interesting, of course, to have both plays, but as for the presence of both being necessary, this strikes me as a mere critical fetish.

And it can have very curious results in practice. Mr Thomson's view of the end of the *Electra* is that Sophocles expects us to put two and two together, piecing out his play, so to speak, by what we recall of the *Choephoroe*. He does not *tell* us that the Erinyes are waiting, and that in ten minutes' time they will pounce; but that is what he intends. This is how Mr Thomson expresses it:

So far as the future of Orestes is concerned, he leaves the audience to draw their own conclusions from the *Oresteia*. But what does the future hold in store for Electra? Her hope has been fulfilled, she has won her deliverance, but the result is her utter desolation:

> O Curse of this sad House, unconquerable,
> How wide thy vision! Even that which seemed
> Well-ordered, safe beyond the reach of harm,
> Thou hast brought down with arrows from afar,
> And left me desolate, stripped of all I loved.[1]

If my own experience is at all typical, many readers of Mr Thomson must have paused at this point and reached for their Sophocles in bewilderment. How could they ever have overlooked such a speech! If Electra really uttered those words (how odd that they should somehow have slipped past one!), then further argument is superfluous. Of course Mr Thomson is right; of course Mr Sheppard is right. There is assuredly no happy ending where the heroine can use words like those. Then suddenly one realizes what has happened. Mr Thomson has made a neat transition from the Sophoclean play to the Aeschylean. The Sophoclean

[1] *Aeschylus and Athens* (1941), p. 359.

Electra did not speak those words. They were spoken by her counterpart[1] in the *Choephoroe*. In the Sophoclean play Electra is silent during the last few moments. The last words she herself spoke in the play were in fierce exhortation to Orestes to put an end to Aegisthus and to toss his corpse to the dogs. But this makes no difference to Mr Thomson. As the Sophoclean *Electra* finishes he thinks that we should be hearing the echoes, not of these parting words of Electra in our play, but of what another Electra once said in another. Could any view be in more glaring negation of our common experience of dramas? Could any view underline more piquantly the risks to which a critic is exposed when he accepts as his guiding principle the idea that Sophocles' dramas are being partly written by Aeschylus?

Secondly, the questions raised by this play are essentially technical, not moral. Critics have made efforts to save the play by the moralistic approach; that, at bottom, is Mr Bowra's endeavour; but this line of defence seems hopeless. It is true, of course, that Sophocles has eased the problem by making Clytaemnestra so vile; she is so outside all reasonable sympathy that we skirt by many an obstacle that lurked in this dangerous theme. As Mr Bowra has expressed it, she does not really count as a mother; and because she does not count in that way the killing loses some of its shockingness. What happens is that we lose sight of matricide and think unconsciously in terms of homicide. This is part of the truth, but not all of it. Clytaemnestra, when all is said, is a mother, and we never fully lose our sense of that fact. Her repulsiveness helps our acceptance, but more important causes

---

[1] Or perhaps not even by her counterpart—perhaps by Clytaemnestra. The attribution is still under discussion.

are working. A dramatist could have kept her revolting, and yet by certain methods in the treatment have brought out the full horror of the killing. Mr Bowra, try as he will, cannot really solve the problem by ethics. He is constantly driven to posit disturbances that are not in the play: the killing of a mother is an ugly business, no matter how bad she may have been, so the slayers must, somehow, have suffered—'what has happened has been undeniably painful', there have been 'wounds' that 'will take time to heal'.[1] Mr Bowra's 'woulds' and 'musts' show very clearly the nature of his commentary—'the conflict that *must* arise',[2] 'Orestes, then, *would* be faced . . .'.[3] This is not lawful critical procedure: we have no right to supplement a drama—to supply what we feel must have been present (though not a sign of it is anywhere shown), to add substance where in the drama is blankness. 'Blankness', here, is precisely the word, for Sophocles has left unsuggested those conflicts that would really have ensued. That has been his technique from the outset, his purpose from the start of the play.

What, then, is to be our verdict, in the upshot? If Sophocles has suppressed so much, must not the result be an inferior drama? Yes, in a sense it must; but there is no real occasion for panic. Mr Kitto will have no half measures. If a moral problem is raised and then the dramatist puts it by, 'he must excuse us', says Mr Kitto, 'if we take no further interest either in his characters or in his poetry', and he must give us leave, ever after, to doubt 'his artistic integrity'.[4] But this is a little extreme. In any case, the answer to it is

[1] C. M. Bowra, *op. cit.*, p. 257.   [2] *Ibid.*, p. 230.
[3] *Ibid.*, p. 220.   [4] *Op. cit.*, p. 129.

easy: Sophocles did not bring the moral problem into focus; the moral problem was what he suppressed. It is not that he could not see it (that might have been the case with Pindar). He was not inclined to make it his theme. That was perhaps reprehensible of him, but who are we to repine? He has given us a remarkable play. It is stronger, in some ways, than the *Antigone*. Electra is an extraordinary study—Sophocles is *closer* to feelings than before. And the skill with which our curiosities are whetted, the superb drawing out of the material, the absolute command of the timing—all these are things to be prized. Sophocles aims lower than he could: but how much occasion for our thanks! The *Electra* is not a great tragedy, is not even (in a deep way) a tragedy; it is still a play by a very great dramatist. And in what other play of the seven can we so observe the sleights of the Master?

CHAPTER X

SOPHOCLES IMPROVISES: THE *PHILOCTETES*

WE must begin, I think, with the recognition that the story of the wounded exile on Lemnos had somewhat restricted possibilities for drama: that it was, in fact, a dramatic subject of the second rank. It is true that the three great tragedians all came to it, and that it attracted minor tragedians as well. This is not altogether surprising; it was an important myth and many elements in the story had piquancy. All the same, a certain stationariness marks it. The problem it poses is this: whether Philoctetes can or cannot be forced or persuaded or tricked into withdrawing from exile on the island and lending his indispensable aid against Troy. There are momentous issues, plainly, in the background, but issues in the background do not make a drama. The issue in the foreground is the dramatic concern, and I think it must be conceded that, though this is mildly interesting, it is not deeply suffused with suspense. The playwright will need to be on his mettle if this theme is to hold our attention; he will somehow have to adapt and relieve the stationariness if he is to secure changefulness and variety of appeal. In other words, a dramatist who selects Philoctetes for a subject is almost compelled to be ingenious; he is driven into a search for ways and means of supplementing his given material. Sophocles' play has precisely this note; it is by far the most ingenious of his dramas. It was a clever manoeuvre, in the first place, to combine the two missions for help (the legend of the embassy to Philoctetes with the legend of the embassy to Neoptolemus himself[1]) and to make Neoptolemus the assistant of Odysseus. This effected a neat compression of material and opened opportunities, not yet in the story, for sympathetic realization of character. Even so, the subject was difficult—not at all a gift to a dramatist. That stubborn *immobility* was the trouble. The theme can never develop a strong momentum in itself; it needs constant prodding by the dramatist. He cannot leave it to itself (so to speak) for a moment; he has to stimulate it every few pages, think out ways of diversifying the interest, ease it along its path, galvanize it when it flags. It is very instructive, as we read the play, to observe the experienced Sophocles in action—how delicate is his sense of the audience, how promptly he responds to each need, how surely he feels his way.

After some rapid introductory talk, we find ourselves listening to the plan of Odysseus. He cannot approach Philoctetes in person, for the exile has good reason to hate him; indeed, to be recognized by Philoctetes will be fatal as long as Philoctetes has the bow. So Neoptolemus must help; and as persuasion and force will be vain, he must use deceit as his means. There is some parley upon this point: Neoptolemus does not exactly see why force will necessarily fail; nor why Philoctetes need be impervious to argument. He is told flatly by Odysseus that it is so, and, as Odysseus presumably knows best, makes but feeble resistance. Then

---

[1] The prophet Helenus declared that two things must be done: Philoctetes must be brought back from Lemnos, and Neoptolemus must be sent for from Scyros.

Odysseus prepares to depart. He has given Neoptolemus no specific instructions, merely a general plan of action. As he leaves he adds one more thing. If Neoptolemus should get into difficulties, a messenger will be dispatched. He will be none other than their present sentinel and will reappear in the guise of a ship's master. It will be Neoptolemus' duty to listen to him and wait very carefully for cues.

What is the effect so far (we have now reached verse 134 of the play)? If we survey, even cursorily, what has happened, we shall see that there has been a good deal of contrivance. The function of the emissary is clear; he lures our curiosity along, he serves, in a sense, as insurance against a plot that might suddenly droop. Odysseus is setting intricate machinery in motion. (That, at least, is the impression at the moment, and that is what Sophocles, chiefly, is trying for. If we inquire at the end of the play just what was Odysseus' plan, we may find this not very easy to answer.) We have the sensation of complexities ahead. But there are subtler points in the scene. If we inspect the text at all closely we shall realize the careful indefiniteness that marks the major *données* of the play. What precisely is it that Odysseus is after? If we read what he says, and then think, we shall recognize that we have really no idea. Is the bow the true object of the mission? Or must the bow and its owner be combined? Would it serve to abduct Philoctetes? Is it any use dragging him to Troy? And suppose, when he got there, he continued refractory? Must he, at some time or other, be persuaded? Is his willingness finally essential? It is hopeless to try to answer these questions—the scene leaves them in utter confusion. If we gather and assess our impressions we have to set them out somehow like this. The bow seems to be the grand object. It must be procured or Troy never will be sacked (68-9); the problem of problems, accordingly, is by stealth to get possession of those arms (77-8); only with those arrows will Troy be taken (113). One or two phrases seem to suggest that Philoctetes is to be captured in person, and it seems also to be implied that, when captured, he is to be haled willy-nilly to Troy (112). Neoptolemus at this point begins to wonder how he himself fits into the picture, and is told by Odysseus not to worry: he is still foreordained to be taker of Troy—but only in conjunction with these arms. So the arms, once again, seem capital, and to what extent they can be separated from their owner is a dubious question once more. A good deal of this seems deliberate. Sophocles, dramatist to his finger-tips, needs some 'play' here for freedom of movement. These ambiguities were essential. (An audience, of course, would not note them.) It means that, as the play progresses, Sophocles can give himself elbow room for fruitful developments. Depending as he must, here, on inspirations, it would have been fatal to tie his hands at the outset. He must have opportunity for happy variations—unexpected turns and twists in the plot—and a rigid formulation of the mission would have robbed him of half of these chances; in fact, it would have quenched the play. Bit by bit it will grow clearer just what has to be done if Troy is ever to be captured; it will become as clear as Sophocles wishes it to be. All this is playwright's business, and the grand object of it all is to keep the drama afloat.

That is to say: there is no reason whatever to assume that those vaguenesses I have mentioned have a meaning—that they signify a deep design, that if we follow out all their

o 199

implications carefully we shall reach the idea of the play. It is Mr Bowra's view that we shall; and as, again, an important principle is involved, the view calls for brief inspection and analysis.

Mr Bowra's reading derives, in essence, from that deep-seated critical belief that great dramatists are always profound. A play may seem relatively superficial, but let us only dig deep enough and somewhere we shall strike on a meaning: it was this belief that turned so much criticism of Shakespeare into a glorified treasure-hunt. The 'central idea' of *Twelfth Night*, the 'inner meaning' of the *Two Gentlemen of Verona*: a Shakespearian play had to be gossamer indeed to baulk the searchers for 'intention'. The *Philoctetes* has more ballast than these comedies, and certainly if significance can legitimately be found we should always be grateful to find it. But the game should be played within rules; and I have suggested already that one of the principal rules that apply is that dramatists *do not tuck away meanings*. Where would be the sense in the method? Dramatists give their whole minds to expression; that is problem enough in itself; to conceive them as busy *concealing* is to brand the whole tribe as eccentric.

Mr Bowra's image of the *Philoctetes* is of a play with a hidden key. The key is well planted in the drama; we have to wait until the play is nearly half over before there is a chance of our finding it; and then we are lucky to identify it. Briefly, it is the oracle of Helenus, recounted to Neoptolemus by the merchant captain. Odysseus waylaid this prophet, then exhibited him, bound, to the host. Among other things Helenus said that Troy would never be taken until Philoctetes had been *persuaded* to come. Here, says Mr Bowra, is the key. The prophet gave specific advice; but Odysseus chose to follow it only in a general way, or in ways that suited his own ideas; and all this trouble has been the result. Naturally Philoctetes proves difficult and the whole embassage faces failure. Not until they repair their error and take pains to be accurate in obedience can they hope for the success of their mission.

So the meaning of the play is revealed. Sophocles deliberately left us in the dark. It was as if he muddled us by intention—concealing in the earlier part of the play the true nature of its structure and ideas. Then in the fulness of time—'with the technique of his ripe old age'[1]—he causes the obscurity to clear, and we see what the play is about.

I think that Mr Bowra is completely mistaken in believing that Sophocles ever worked in this way, least of all when his technique was advanced. It would have been a muddled technique. A dramatist does not give a sense of illusion by bewildering the audience itself. Suppose he wishes to show obscure passions and characters wandering in the dark; he is no dramatist if he attempts to do this by leaving us to grope about in a blackness. But are these characters so much in the dark? Is Odysseus deeply at fault in not adhering strictly to the oracle? Certainly he seems to have been very inattentive, but such laziness is pervasive in the drama. It is most interesting to note that when it comes to the point Philoctetes is equally in a fog. He has heard the exact terms of the oracle; he accepts them unquestionably for authentic. Yet when Odysseus taunts him later with his dispensableness as a person—'I have the bow; that is all I need; you may stay where you are if you care to'[2]—it does not occur to

---

[1] C. M. Bowra, *op. cit.*, p. 264.   [2] Vv. 1055 ff.

Philoctetes to give the immediate and obvious reply. He, too, is quite prepared for the moment to believe that someone else may handle the bow and that his presence may not really be required. If the oracle were all-important could Sophocles have risked such an incident? But this incident is characteristic. In not one passage of the drama does Sophocles *make the point* that Odysseus has been seriously at fault in the way he has taken the oracle, and that this is essentially why things go wrong.

This is not to deny for a moment that disaster did, in fact, often result from a careless handling of oracles. Mr Bowra gives cases to prove it. Men sometimes did not ask enough or they interpreted according to their fancies; or they exceeded what the oracle had bidden; or they neglected some part of the instructions. It still does not matter for our play. The theory of oracles is not so precise that no further pointing is needed.[1] Here, the blurring of the edges was easy. We are not warned about the misreading of the oracle. It can seem to us that the envoys, at any given moment, are working within allowable limits—are following, within reason, their instructions. That is the definite impression of the drama and that is the impression by which we must abide. The authoritative text of the oracle when it comes has little corrective value—because it is so weak in the values of drama. (And what dramatist would have postponed the vital clue to so late a point in his play?) When Odysseus and Neoptolemus debate procedure, with Neoptolemus favouring persuasion, and Odysseus says, 'there is no chance whatever of persuading him' (103), we are dramatically compelled to accept this. We could only discount Odysseus' conviction

[1] See pp. 171 ff.

if at a later stage in the drama something occurred that had the effect of exploding it: if by some means it were made quite clear to us that he had been proceeding on false lines from the outset. Then and then only would we be entitled to believe that he gravely misinterpreted the oracle and that he is paying the penalty for this fault. But his conviction is never exploded. From beginning to end, the drama never makes capital out of Odysseus' disobedience of instructions.

As for the general effect of this opening scene, it was clearly Sophocles' purpose that it should leave us properly expectant. We have the sense of developments pending, of a plot getting under way. Presently we see the first results of the strategy laid down by Odysseus. Everything goes according to plan. Neoptolemus plays his part so well that by v. 468 Philoctetes is heard begging earnestly to be taken on board. Neoptolemus still plays his part well, displaying no particular interest. By v. 526 he has given his somewhat casual consent. At v. 538 he and Philoctetes are seen about to enter the cave, the overjoyed exile having invited him to inspect his humble abode before they leave. It is interesting —and also a little amusing—to note what these developments mean. Mr Bowra says that Odysseus erred by not following the oracle closely, and that this error is the reason why all his planning comes to naught. But his planning has not come to naught; on the contrary, it has been quite successful. Philoctetes has been trapped by guile, he has proved the easiest of victims. The problem with which the play began is now, to all intents and purposes, over. Philoctetes will pack up his goods, will gratefully board the ship, and then at the appropriate moment will be neatly relieved of his bow; or will be coaxed into acquiescence, according to the policy pursued. On the terms laid down by the drama, success has now crowned the plot.

The next step, therefore, is obvious—Sophocles has it already planned. He must quickly thrust out into the open again a play reaching port too soon. Accordingly, no sooner have the two men turned to enter the cave than the Merchant appears on the scene, and presently is retailing his complex story of malice and pursuit and conspiracy. What good can this possibly do? The intervention of the Merchant is not necessary; on the contrary, it is worse than superfluous. It has two principal results; the first is to make Philoctetes very nervous; the second is to render him still more eager to put himself into Neoptolemus' care. Neither result adds anything to what has already been accomplished. Philoctetes is already resolved; the inopportune arrival of the Merchant can only upset him and make more likely some possible slip. In a word, this is not very good drama. One sees, of course, what Sophocles is about; he is keeping his play on the move. It is clever improvisation; it fills up a space with material; it keeps our interest from flagging. We have the *illusion* that something is being furthered—actually, nothing is. Odysseus must have been a veritable bungler if this was the best he could do. If we took the matter seriously at all we should have to judge him a novice, or else a man so bemused with contrivance that within ten minutes he has his own plot in a coil by sheer superfluity of planning. Of course nothing of this is in question. It is Sophocles who is here the contriver—with a thoroughly unsound piece of action, that nevertheless keeps his drama afloat.

At the end of it we are where we began. Philoctetes presses for haste; Neoptolemus on the other hand—for some reason—seems now reluctant to leave. He objects that the winds are unfavourable. Perhaps it is an early twinge of his conscience, perhaps there is no significance in the remark. At all events he agrees, and they set about preparations for boarding. These give Sophocles the opportunity for his next brief theme or dramatic resource; accordingly (not without some awkwardness, as Wilamowitz noted) he makes the transition to the matter of the bow. Neoptolemus helps Philoctetes with his packing: what necessaries must he take? There is the herb that assuages his wound; some arrows left lying about. So we come by degrees to the bow—and the audience watch in suspense. 'So this is the famous bow!' It is an age-old trick, but a good one, this device of 'Missed by an Inch'; and here, as well, we may see how important for the interest it was that the exact requirements of the oracle should have been left a little obscure. All our attention is now on the bow—will Neoptolemus suddenly snatch it? Is this the critical moment? He asks reverently for permission to handle it, and the permission is readily given; then he seems as if moved by some compunction; in the end his hands barely touch it. Philoctetes gives him friendly assurance that some day he will have the privilege of trying the famous bow. So from moment to moment, cleverly inventive, Sophocles eases his play on its way.[1]

At this point he still had strong reserves, and the physical agony of Philoctetes in particular was something that he could exploit to advantage. In addition, by the time this stage was reached a truer movement in the drama had begun. At v. 806 we have the first unequivocal sign of a change in the

[1] I do not mean that the play lacks planning, but that the very planning is a kind of improvisation.

mood of Neoptolemus: he says his heart has for some time been heavy, brooding over Philoctetes' woes. This is something in which we easily believe; sooner or later the frank, impressionable Neoptolemus must rebel against the role that has been assigned him; his better feelings, sooner or later, will be uncontrollable, his inherent decency must out. And now for the first time (we may say) the play acquires a momentum of its own—moves by its intrinsic forces instead of being guided and pushed. Given the natures of these three men a conflict is bound to develop. Yet the theme is still awkward to handle. The contest soon gives ominous signs of settling into permanent deadlock, and we have the sensation, before the finish, that only some miracle will break it. As it turns out, a miracle does. Many pages have been written about the use here of the *deus ex machina*; it is said that it is not really what it seems, that in any case Sophocles did not need it, that it is far from betraying a weakness. It is true that Sophocles brings it in skilfully and gives it an appearance of propriety. It serves to round out the myth. Heracles himself is not an intruder; he has a personal concern in the case and his intervention is in a sense justified by friendship. Besides, he does more than merely cut knots; he advises, illuminates, consoles. All this, and perhaps more, we may say; still, the *deus ex machina* remains. The god intervenes in the action, because no issue is visible without him. The drama, as such, is bogged down—that is the plain fact of the matter; its own motive forces are exhausted, the conflict has lapsed into stalemate, and something desperate must be done. Sophocles' *deus ex machina* is an admirable example of the type; if such expedients are ever to be resorted to, then here, certainly, is a model to follow. But its essential nature is unchanged; its function is to engineer a conclusion that without it could never have come.[1]

I think, then, that in the *Philoctetes* we see Sophocles as more of an opportunist than is customary with him in his writing. The theme is essentially inferior; he has to rise to its challenge, give life and diversity to a story that had no special promise in itself. His achievement, of course, is remarkable, and it is not as if he were solely concerned with eking out the limitations of the plot. The treatment is rich in humanity. The warm portraiture of Neoptolemus (the discomfort of the young man in his role, the visible growth in him of self-knowledge); the presentment of Philoctetes' despairs (so impressive in their depths, and so unexpected in their shadings)—these are notable accomplishments in imaginative sympathy. Yet even these, fine as they are, hardly bring into existence great drama. Every step by Neoptolemus towards his better self means a draining of the forces of the play. The dramatic energy diminishes with every move towards a reconcilement. As Neoptolemus and Philoctetes 'make it up', the drama is fast running down. And the moods of Philoctetes himself—interesting as they are within their range—can only stabilize still further a situation already only too stable. We reach a state of equalization, in which the energies are so evenly diffused that no further progress is possible. That is what always threatened to happen to this story, and that is what is fatal in the end. Odysseus, it is true, is still there—still intermittently present —but he has lost nearly all his initial impressiveness, and

[1] Of course, Sophocles might have made Philoctetes retire, then re-enter a changed man, *à la* Ajax. Even then, there would have been no difference in principle.

does little but dodge in and out making ineffectual protests. At the end he is a supernumerary, Sophocles dropping him perfunctorily some distance before the finish of the play.

There remain those 'touches of nature' that are such a mark of this drama, and, without doubt, they truly distinguish it. Philoctetes' eager inquiries as Neoptolemus tells of the host (the great Ajax dead and gone! but surely not the son of Tydeus? and what of his old friend, Nestor?); the pictures of the exile's life, his cave, his lonely days; his final farewell to the place that by habit is now part of his being: these are all memorable things and deserve our unstinted praise. Yet they are incidentals in the drama, and it is not without significance that they abound in this play which, of all seven, finds Sophocles fighting hardest for interest.

Let us pass to one or two questions of interpretation.

What of the Chorus here? Is it really a 'delicate instrument'? The context was awkward for a Chorus; the play is so realistic in tone that it could easily be felt as an interloper. Has Sophocles surmounted this difficulty, 'welding'[1] his Chorus with the action in what we may take as a new triumph of his art? It is not to be denied that the treatment is ingenious, or that these sailors of Neoptolemus have among them a kind of mind. They are bidden to stand by at the outset—to be ready with whatever they can think of may support the young man in his difficult task. And they are serviceable in this duty. Towards the end, when alone with Philoctetes, they even take it upon themselves to deliver a lecture, reproving the stubborn man for his conduct; and when their homilies fail they can show a touch of

[1] H. D. F. Kitto, *op. cit.*, p. 305.

human impatience. 'Leave me, begone', he says; and they reply that they are very willing to do so; only for his sake have they stayed so long. There are here, then, faint glimmerings of personality. As for the lyricism, it is markedly reduced, and what remains of it is cleverly adapted to the fluctuations of the theme. There is, therefore, very much to approve. It seems to me, all the same, excessive to regard the achievement with wonder. Sophocles manages this Chorus *nearly* as well as, in the circumstances, one could properly expect; but its function, after all, is slight and its presence seems faintly vestigial. What exactly does this Chorus accomplish? It helps us to feel for Philoctetes; but cannot we feel for him by ourselves? It helps us to understand Neoptolemus; but are our own imaginations so slow? It supplies needful—or useful—pauses, and its presence decorates the stage. I doubt whether we can say much more. The Chorus in such a play as this is obviously in decline; its heyday is clearly long past. Sophocles puts it through the old paces with all his customary dexterity—and makes neat adjustments in the paces. But what he gives is like an echo of the past. This Chorus is a kind of reminiscence; its office is virtually gone.

I say that Sophocles manages this Chorus nearly as well as one had a right to expect of him, for in one place he appears to have been guilty of a quite extraordinary lapse. The Chorus know what is afoot; they are well versed in what is proceeding; and they have shown by their interjections that they are trying to forward the plot. Then at v. 676 they are left alone and break into a remarkable song. It is full of deep sympathy for Philoctetes. Of no other mortal but one have they heard so piteous a story: how, unsinning, he was left here to perish. They dilate on his loneliness and suffering, on his various hardships and privations. Then they say, 'all this is over':

> But now, after those troubles, he shall be happy and mighty at the last; for he hath met with the son of a noble race, who in the fulness of many months bears him on sea-cleaving ship to his home, haunt of Malian nymphs, and to the banks of the Spercheius; where, above Oeta's heights, the lord of the brazen shield drew near to the gods, amid the splendour of the lightnings of his sire.[1]

No one knows better than the Chorus that there is no intention of taking Philoctetes to his homeland. What are we to make of this song?

One way of interpretation lies open and a number of critics have chosen it. It is to suppose that as the Chorus are singing Neoptolemus and Philoctetes reappear. From that point the Chorus resume their role as assistant conspirators, and are again in complicity with their master, singing of a journey and a happy ending of which they believe not one word.

Let us think what this reading implies. It implies that at a certain point in their ode the Chorus made an abrupt *volte-face*. Their initial mood was genuine—there is not the slightest question of that. Then, at a signal, they are able to wrench themselves from this mood, and resume the cloak of hypocrisy. There is no overt hint in the text, of course, that they are doing anything of the kind. We deduce that this must be what is happening because it seems the only way to make sense of the ode.

There are insuperable difficulties in this view. Think only

[1] Vv. 718-29, trans. Jebb.

of the sort of light it casts on the character of the Chorus itself. It is one thing for the Chorus to assist the conspiracy by occasional intervention or comment; it is another thing for the Chorus to debase an ode by suddenly turning it to trickery and falsehood. This could only strike us as indecent behaviour. But how could the Chorus have done it? They were carried away by their feeling, borne along on a strong tide of emotion. How did they bring all this to a stop, change the key of their lyrical outburst, shift from reality to pretence in an instant? We have only to ponder it for a moment to see that the thing is absurd. As I say, there is no *rift* in the ode, no clue to such a change in the text; and really there is no way in which a change so drastic could be indicated in a song.

I do not think any reader will doubt that Sophocles would make heavy sacrifices for an ode, and that often while he was writing an ode the play receded a little from his vision. At all events it is very easy to observe that he did not tie his Choruses to their parts. Sometimes they are well within their nominal roles, at times they are a little outside them. This ode that we are considering is exceptional in degree. The sailors would have run quite true to type if they had been mildly absent-minded; it is because their absent-mindedness is, in this case, so staggering that we are suddenly pulled up short. The latitude that Sophocles habitually allowed himself has for once become extreme.

A second passage raises a similar question, but this time (so to speak) in reverse. I do not know that verses 1055-80 have been thought to contain a problem, but it seems to me that they do. The bow is now in the possession of the conspirators, and Philoctetes himself has been bound. Then, suddenly, Odysseus gives orders to release him. The passage continues as follows:

Odysseus. Yes, release him, lay no finger upon him more—let him stay here. Indeed, we have no further need of thee, now that these arms are ours; for Teucer is there to serve us, well-skilled in this craft, and I, who deem that I can wield this bow no whit worse than thou, and point it with as true a hand. What need, then, of thee? Pace thy Lemnos, and joy be with thee! We must be going. And perchance thy treasure will bring to me the honour which ought to have been thine own.

Philoctetes. Ah, unhappy that I am, what shall I do? Shalt *thou* be seen among the Argives graced with the arms that are mine?

Odysseus. Bandy no more speech with me—I am going.

Philoctetes. Son of Achilles, wilt thou, too, speak no more to me, but depart without a word?

Odysseus (to Neoptolemus.) Come on! Do not look at him, generous though thou art, lest thou mar our fortune.

Philoctetes (to Chorus). Will ye also, friends, indeed leave me thus desolate, and show no pity?

Chorus. This youth is our commander; whatsoever he saith to thee, that answer is ours also.

Neoptolemus (to Chorus). I shall be told by my chief that I am too soft-hearted; yet tarry ye here, if yon man will have it so, until the sailors have made all ready on board, and we have offered our prayers to the gods. Meanwhile, perhaps, he may come to a better mind concerning us. So we two will be going, and ye, when we call you, are to set forth with speed.[1]

We know by now the exact terms of the oracle, and though the bow, naturally, is still the centre of interest, it seems at this stage to be generally taken for granted that Philoctetes must go in person to Troy. Odysseus himself seems to hold this view, for we have heard him declare (982) not only that

[1] Vv. 1055-80, trans. Jebb.

the bow will not be returned to Philoctetes, but that Philoctetes must go along with it when they sail. Then, after the frenzy and the binding of Philoctetes, comes the surprising passage just quoted. Odysseus now says that the bow is enough; why should they trouble further about its owner? Nobody objects to this view on the ground that Philoctetes is essential; the thought does not even occur to Philoctetes himself. Theoretically he was in a position to laugh at them, but instead he is thrown into a panic.

What is to be made of the passage? Is it a somewhat pointless transitional episode or has it a dramatic meaning? I would suggest (with hesitation) that it has dramatic meaning, and that what Odysseus is supposed to be doing is enticing Philoctetes by a bait. Philoctetes responds at once. He has an agonizing picture of Odysseus flaunting the bow or of some other hero among the Argives achieving the honour that should be rightfully his. He is plunged into fearful distraction: what should he do—give in, or wait in torture on the island while another wins renown with his bow? Odysseus sees his distress and tactfully leaves him to writhe in it: 'Bandy no more words; I am off.' Philoctetes turns imploringly to Neoptolemus, who is also making as if to depart. Then he directs his appeal to the Chorus. It is almost as if Neoptolemus has 'caught on'—has detected Odysseus' manoeuvre—for he gives his sailors permission to stay, half blaming himself for his weakness. It is as if they were being left on purpose to prod Philoctetes further, and perhaps (as he is already in such a state) to accept his capitulation.

I would make little effort to defend the last part of the reading I have offered; there is, of course, no clear indication that Neoptolemus is not taking Odysseus seriously. But as for Odysseus' own part in the affair: the reversal of policy is so marked, the change so abrupt and surprising that any audience would be struck. They would certainly be on the alert for a meaning; and the panic of Philoctetes is no fancy —not something that one imagines or deduces—it is there, most decidedly, in the text. In other words, I do not think that we are guilty of the documentary fallacy if we interpret Odysseus' behaviour as a ruse; such a reading is not merely inference, it is really suggested by the text. Yet it is hard to feel confidence in the reading; and this, again, seems to me interesting and to reflect something typical in Sophocles. It is as if occasionally he has had an intention that he has not managed quite clearly to convey. (I have suggested that this may be true of certain difficulties in the *Ajax* and the *Antigone*.) It is as if occasionally he were defeated in expression, as if occasionally he were reaching for something on which his fingers cannot quite close—the exhibition of some shade of conduct, the fixing of some subtlety in motive. He had powerful resources, in all conscience; yet for such objects as I have just tried to indicate perhaps he needed still other resources—not so much more delicate instruments as instruments of a different design. There is nothing more interesting in Sophocles than this *explorative* tinge to his methods—this sense of a reaching out, as if even his magnificent equipment became eventually too limited for his purposes, as if even his rich technique did not quite suffice, in the end, for his wants.[1]

[1] The interpretation of vv. 1055-80 that I have advanced struck Jebb as a possible view. 'Odysseus must be conceived as merely using a last threat, which, he hopes, may cause Philoctetes to yield.' (*Sophocles: The Philoctetes* [1890], p. xxviii.) But Jebb half contradicts this by his note on v. 1052:

Finally, there is the kind of view that sees the whole play as a parable: Mr Edmund Wilson's theory of it is an example.[1] Mr Wilson thinks that its dominant 'symbols' come back to us with a curious insistence and affect us as oddly familiar. 'Why do we enter with scarcely a stumble into the situation of people who are preoccupied with a snake-bite that lasts for ever and a weapon that cannot fail?' Mr Wilson's answer, in effect, is that a symbolic correspondence exists between the story of this wound and this bow and a poignant modern situation. Often men of genius arise who from injuries imagined or suffered, or from some psychological quirk, are strangely ill at ease in society. In a spiritual way they are like Philoctetes, and often, like him, they are outlawed. Yet society needs these men, these cranky embittered geniuses, and it is vaguely conscious of the need. Sometimes it can lure them back, bring about a reconciliation. Genius has to be treated tenderly; it will see through tricks in a flash, but it will respond to understanding. So by tactful application of sympathy the wound may sometimes be healed, and society regain for its uses the bow.

Mr Wilson has other theses about genius that need not be scrutinized here: as that it forms a natural pair with disease and is normally accompanied by defect. He also has theses about Sophocles, some of which we have noted before: as 'Odysseus is resigned to Philoctetes carrying his point by staying in Lemnos.' As I say, no real confidence is possible. Mr Harsh (*A Handbook of Classical Drama* [1944], p. 146) says it is obvious that Odysseus is dissembling. It does not seem obvious to Neoptolemus, and it is certainly not obvious to Philoctetes. That is why (in default of a broad wink) it would have been so hard to make it obvious to an audience. This technical *impasse* had a fatal attraction for Sophocles; one would have thought that his experiences in the *Ajax* would have warned him.

[1] *The Wound and the Bow* (1941), pp. 272 ff.

that Sophocles specialized in psychological derangements and was particularly quick in detecting 'fixations'. Philoctetes is certainly embittered, but, apart from his natural resentfulness, shows little trace, surely, of mental aberration. His behaviour is very predictable; his obstreperousness causes much bother, but even Odysseus and Neoptolemus have to admit that in the circumstances it is only too normal.

Mr Wilson's reading of the play is enticing; at all events it provokes interesting thoughts; and anyone coming to it apart from the play would, no doubt, think it very attractive and plausible. But Mr Wilson is always to be watched when he is revealing the deep import of a work. It is always advisable, before one succumbs, to have another close look at the work. In this case he has not achieved his interpretation without slightly twisting the facts. For example, it is rather essential to his parable that the man of genius should be softened by sympathy: that he should consent to re-enter the general life because he feels he is at last understood. But in this respect the play is rather awkward; Neoptolemus stands for society and gives Philoctetes his full sympathy; it accomplishes nothing whatever. Philoctetes is understood again by someone; it makes not a particle of difference; he is still resolute to stay where he is. Mr Wilson slurs all this over. He has to minimize the *deus ex machina*, to begin with. He says it 'may of course figure a change of heart which has taken place in Philoctetes as the result of his having found a man who recognizes the wrong that has been done him'.[1] But why should it do any such thing? This is one of Mr Wilson's favourite gambits: it will be observed that what he is really trying to induce us to do is to accept his own

[1] *Op. cit.*, p. 283.

piece of drama for Sophocles'! If Sophocles had wished to show Philoctetes changing through sympathy it was perfectly open to him to show this. As he has so carefully refrained from doing so we can only presume that he had another idea. 'He dissolves Philoctetes' stubbornness';[1] but this is precisely what Neoptolemus does not do. It is because he has not succeeded in doing it that Heracles has to be brought into the play. And why does Mr Wilson import a supernatural influence ('the supernatural influences in Sophocles are often made with infinite delicacy to shade into subjective motivations')[2] to make it clear to Neoptolemus that the bow is no good by itself? There is no mystery whatever about this matter. Neoptolemus has heard the plain words of the oracle; no supernatural influence on him is involved.

There is no apt word for what Mr Wilson has given us in his essay *The Wound and the Bow*. One could call it creative criticism in a half complimentary way. The essay is certainly creative—a most interesting comment on life; but its relation with the *Philoctetes* is tenuous. Mr Wilson does not truly interpret, for, as we have seen, he achieves his parable only at the cost of altering the play.

---

[1] *Op. cit.*, p. 295. [2] *Ibid.*, p. 294.

CHAPTER XI

GRAND FINALE:
THE *OEDIPUS COLONEUS*

THE *Oedipus Coloneus* is often spoken of as if it were a difficult play, troublesome to estimate and appraise: as if one had to brood over it to discover its workings, as if one had to extract its inner secrets by labour.[1] These difficulties seem to me self-created. I would suggest that problems of any kind are singularly absent from this work, and that, if we consider the play as a whole, we shall find the critical situation nearly at its simplest.

Sophocles' problem is easy to see. It is a problem that repeats, in essentials, the problem of the *Philoctetes*, and the methods that Sophocles resorts to are very much the same in type. Here was a theme that attracted him deeply—it was obviously foreordained; and there was an inherent propriety and rightness in his leaving it for a task of old age. Or, if the thought of it occurred to him late, one can still feel the depth of the attraction. Events may have combined to suggest it—a reference in Euripides' *Phoenissae*, a battle a year before at Colonus. There was probably an external impulse, and underneath this again, a strong drawing of personal interest. But how did he feel about the subject as dramatist? His own feeling as a man about Colonus, his Athenian's passion for Athens: these are deep in the fibres of

[1] Cf. H. D. F. Kitto, *op. cit.*, pp. 386 ff.

the play, but they would not have sufficed him for the writing of it. As a dramatist he would have seen promise in the subject, and, above everything, the chance to write one scene that might be made the most memorable in all his dramas. The thought of that scene must have conquered him, but it could not have screened the drawbacks that lay waiting for him in this subject. The chief of all the drawbacks was this, that the theme was not sufficient for a drama. The story of Oedipus' death did not contain stuff for a play, but at the most, however one handled it, for a short, tense sequence of scenes. There was this superb climax in sight, but not much to lead up to the climax. Sophocles' problem, accordingly, was simple: it was merely to stretch out the sequence: to keep the climax in its place and to find some suitable material—episodes or a presentable intrigue—for filling out the middle of the play. 'Filling out' is disrespectful to the central parts of the *Oedipus Coloneus*, yet who will not admit to the feeling, as he watches these scenes in progress, that the main matter has been suspended? That, in effect, is what happens. Nothing else in the drama, of course, comes near its majestic conclusion; but where this conclusion differs from other conclusions is that it is, in essence, the theme of the play. The apotheosis[1] of Oedipus is what the play is about. This was the theme with which we began—of a bourn in a life now reached, of a fulfilment presently to be. All our expectancies are on this; and it is, I think, with a sense of *resumption* that we enter on the final

---

[1] 'Oedipus' passing is no apotheosis. It is not accompanied by storms and thunderbolts' (C. M. Bowra, *op. cit.*, p. 341). No, but it is preceded by thunder and lightnings; and it is more like an apotheosis than it is like anything else for which there is a word.

moments of the drama. In between there has been much that was interesting, much to excite us and stir us. But it was all, in essence, distraction. Now, as we hear the premonitory thunder, we have a sense of returning to the high concern of the play.

I do not think that this describes the drama unfairly.[1] To regard the *Coloneus* in this light is not to accuse its author of feebleness: there is no more feebleness in the *Coloneus* than there is in *The Tempest* or *The Winter's Tale*. Sophocles' verses are as powerful as ever; there is economy and suppleness and variety; the *Coloneus* is a richer play than the *Tyrannus*—there are subtler movements in the thought, the speeches have more of sheer interest; and in sublimity it stands alone. But it is a mistake, in rendering homage, to refuse all admission of weakness: to turn the facts so ingeniously around that every defect becomes a virtue—looseness becoming 'new style', unevenness appearing as 'fluidity'. Mr Kitto will not even let go of 'unity', but, as there is no chance of establishing it formally, establishes it as 'impressionistic', and sees Sophocles as now 'transcending the bounds of his own Aristotelian perfection'.[2] Such an ingenious revaluing of terms can do little good to the *Oedipus Coloneus* and is unfair to the *Oedipus Tyrannus*. The *Coloneus* has its own unique title to greatness, but it is not

[1] Or that there is any real mystery about the matter. It was suggested by Kathleen Freeman ('The Dramatic Technique of the *Oedipus Coloneus*', *Classical Review*, XXXVII [1923], pp. 50-4) that this play traces 'the descending curve of a larger structure not given to us entire'; that it is the final phase of a giant non-existent drama whose shape we can fill in, so to speak, with dotted lines. The peripeteia of this hypothetical drama occurred when Oedipus became convinced of his essential innocence. This seems to me to be making unnecessary exertions to keep the *Coloneus* within some accepted pattern of tragedy.   [2] *Op. cit.*, p. 391.

that of the *Tyrannus*. We need not think of Sophocles' powers as waning; but once more, and for the last time, he does what presumably he had often done before: he makes for the theme that tempts him, not counting the cost too closely. Once again, then, as his theme will not carry him, he is thrown back on brilliant improvisation. He is not, as in the *Tyrannus*, releasing the deep energies of his material; he is deliberately constructing a drama, and supplying what pieces it lacks. He has already an excellent opening and a truly wonderful ending; he has now to furnish a middle. He makes it up with intrigues—for one intrigue will hardly suffice—and with episodes of a varying cast. There are altercations and disputes, confrontations and collisions. There is a minor adventure by the way—the abduction and rescue of the daughters—and other sorts of dramatic action. This sounds in summary a hotch-potch, but Sophocles creates very successfully the illusion of progressive movement. Yet he needs still further material, and it is interesting, if one looks closely, to observe how often in these middle portions he resorts to retrospect and prospect. Our thoughts again and again are drawn back to famed calamities or ahead towards conflicts to be. Ghosts from other tragedies move in the air of the *Coloneus*. The drama is often, so to speak, *in absentia*—exists in echo or intimation. So Sophocles weaves together a plot, cunningly spinning it across that yawning gap in this theme. He does it effectively enough, and throws in largesse of poetry. Nevertheless, it is not insensitive to feel much of this intercalary activity as a skilful marking of time.

Let us review the main phases of the drama. The opening scene is superb. The old blind Oedipus and Antigone have drawn near some sacred grove. The stranger whom they question has hardly begun to name it before Oedipus feels that he has reached his goal. In his words there are suggestions of a mystery. He has come to keep some solemn appointment, the accomplishment of his course is at hand; and some deep, far-spreading significance will mark the ending of his life. It is an opening unique in Sophocles, full of a strange hush and a special kind of suspense. Then the suspense is interrupted; the world begins to break in. The Chorus are fussily horrified at the trespass on holy ground, and for long moments the air resounds with their querulous protests and scoldings. Oedipus is timid and bothered, he has become just an old blind man again, shaken by these unexpected rebukes. Feebly he asks his daughter's advice and feebly totters to a seat. Presently calm is restored.

Then, with Oedipus seated and tranquillized, the retrospects I have mentioned begin. The play starts (so to say) on a series of retreats from the matter at present in hand. There is first the disclosure of identity; next, the brief self-justification; then the arrival of Ismene with her report of recent events and her announcement of impending trouble. Then Oedipus has his retrospect, giving his own version of how he was driven from Thebes. (He has already told us what he has owed in the interval to his daughters.) The drama quietens for a moment as the Chorus intervene with instructions about the rites and ceremonies at the shrine. Then, before Theseus enters, we have one further retrospect as the Chorus, rather tactlessly inquisitive, take it upon themselves to rake up the most painful past: they feel that, in fairness to themselves, they cannot forgo this unprecedented opportunity of hearing the truth of that ancient tale.

It is rather interesting to note that we are now at v. 550 of the play—very nearly a third of the way through; and up to this point we have been going steadily backwards. In part the retrospects have had the purpose of filling in the background of the story; in part (as in the case of the last) they are hardly necessary for that and perform no real duty in the play except to be interesting in themselves. Now Theseus enters and the drama livens; a bustling activity begins. The grove becomes a general rendezvous for all who have business—and there are many—with Oedipus. It is a little surprising, when we reflect on it, that he should choose to stay and meet these people. Theseus leaves it to him: he may remain with the citizens of Colonus or he may put himself at once under the protection of Theseus himself. A little hesitantly, as if fearing to offend, Oedipus elects to stay where he is: he says that on this spot he must get the better of those who have wronged him. It is Sophocles' pretext, of course, for securing the continuance of the drama. But the mood of Oedipus himself is interesting. It is often suggested that the deep design beneath all these middle scenes was to show Oedipus increasing steadily in stature.[1] I do not myself detect this 'basic rhythm', this regular and continuous progression. The play is now well advanced, and the stature of Oedipus has, if anything, diminished. As Theseus prepares to depart, Oedipus falls into what may fairly be described as a panic. He is assailed by feverish anxieties about the measures to be taken for his safety. He is quite fussy in his apprehensions—for these moments just a nervous old man who has made a venturesome decision

---

[1] Cf. Maurice Croiset (*Œdipe-Roi de Sophocle* [1931], p. 239): 'Plus l'action se développe, plus la grandeur morale d'Œdipe se fait sentir.'

and now requires assurances from all and sundry that he is not plunging headlong into folly. Then we have the great poem in praise of Colonus and Attica, and after that the entry of Creon. There is plenty of vigour in Oedipus' rebuke.[1] Yet it is difficult to feel that it is Oedipus who is in control of the situation here. Creon, of course, is quite impervious to scoldings and knows that force is on his side. Presently Oedipus is backing away and turning in appeal to his friends. The contest becomes a squabble which seems likely to continue indefinitely. Creon passes from rudeness to threats and from threats to physical violence. Oedipus is dragged hither and thither. The uproar suddenly ceases as Theseus himself comes back.

Oedipus now withdraws a little from the centre while Creon and Theseus talk. Theseus addresses a very strong remonstrance to the Theban, but is careful not to make it too strong, and is especially punctilious in distinguishing between Thebes and her erring son. (The careful exclusion of Thebes from blame is amusing; Sophocles' mind is not wholly on his drama.) Creon is equally diplomatic in rejoinder and is polite in his references to Athens. The exchange makes very good reading—only, what a distance we are at this point from the theme with which we began! We may say much the same, indeed, of the great speech of Oedipus which follows: his splendid apology for his life. He could not have given this

---

[1] It is piquant also in its thought. What hurts Oedipus is the deplorable *mistiming* in all that he has had to endure. In the days immediately following the dreadful discovery he would have accepted expulsion with gratitude, but at that time Creon would do nothing. Then when he had to some extent recovered from the shock and was taking up his life again, down comes banishment upon him. Now his one desire is to stay where he is, and Creon comes to pluck him back.

before. He had to come up from the depths, to regain detachment and clarity, and see the whole story in perspective. Now he commands a view and has confidence in his own assessment. His self-justification is deeply moving; it is also an intellectual pleasure to listen to this long-meditated defence. Yet the ground he re-travels is old. Once more, we are in the region of retrospect, are retreating, in a sense, from this drama. The incident of the abducted daughters pulls us sharply back to the present; rescuers are dispatched and the children of Oedipus are restored. But this adventure is in essence (surely) just another way of marking time in the drama. So, clearly, are the lengthy courtesies between Theseus and Oedipus which follow. (Critics who acclaim the *Oedipus Coloneus* in the same breath with the *Tyrannus* should mark well these patches of text, where the play, so to speak, is at a standstill. Try to find them in the *Tyrannus*! It is drama, drama all the way in the *Tyrannus*; no loiterings or dawdlings there.) One cannot speak in quite these terms of the Polyneices scene. Here is a dramatic confrontation indeed! Yet functionally it is a gripping *interlude*, or not very much more than that. There is, no doubt, a sense of power in the silence, and then the tirade, of the father; but are there very sure grounds for believing that 'on the essential issue between Polyneices and the gods Oedipus has spoken the final word'?[1] His denunciation is all too human in the dominant motives that inspire it. As for power—Oedipus has power because it has suddenly been conferred on him by accident. By accident (or divine bestowal) he finds himself in a position to utter a fiat; by saying a yea or a nay he can settle issues of shattering importance. The most insignificant

[1] C. M. Bowra, *op. cit.*, p. 331.

of beings would be powerful (many insignificant beings have been) when lifted to a station like that. All that Oedipus does is to make the fullest use of his chances, allowing his resentments free sway. He stands pat, is hard, unforgiving: a less noble Oedipus than any we have seen. It may be that the future is settled and that, in a sense, all Oedipus is doing is taking his own prescribed place in the pattern. But that does not oblige us to feel enthusiasm for this Oedipus who curses and taunts. We are not given, actually, a clear lead in the matter—not guided in our responses by the drama. There is at least no very strong reason why we should not pay due heed to Antigone and take our cue, in some measure, from her when she tries to soften and appease. Polyneices perhaps deserved no forgiveness; perhaps forgiveness would have been impossible and wrong. It is difficult, all the same, to feel that Oedipus has won laurels from the scene or added notably to his 'grandeur morale'.

At all events, we find ourselves at this point near the end of the long preliminaries—for, in essence, that is surely what they have been. The scene for which the play was written is at hand. The sky darkens, thunder is heard; and now at last we have an Oedipus who, amid all the circumstances of grandeur, seems in his own nature and life to fit them. The man whom the gods so hunted stands ready for their weird *amende*.

It would have been good if we could have been left awed and stilled by the Messenger's account of the passing. It is not, I think, doing homage to a modern shibboleth to feel that Sophocles unduly spins out the ending. Antigone and Ismene have really nothing to say and they say it to the tune of too many verses.

The problem of the *Coloneus* is just the problem of assessment. As I say, there are no problems of detail that provide any exercise for the mind. If we look, we can see that there are inconsistencies in Oedipus' account of what happened at Thebes. He first says (427 ff.) that when he was banished his sons lifted no finger to save him; then he says (599 ff.) that he was driven out by his own flesh and blood; then he says (1354 ff.) that Polyneices expelled him. These are nearly imperceptible shifts, and I could suggest that it is extremely doubtful whether Sophocles himself was acutely aware of them. When Oedipus is denouncing Polyneices, it would have had a very weak effect if he had split hairs and minced his words; 'drove your own father into exile'—what else *can* he say in the circumstances? It is by no means necessary to the drama that we should know exactly what happened; it is better that we should not know, so that the facts may remain conveniently adaptable. I do not think that the problem is deeper.

Finally, there is the patriotic suffusion. This is not necessarily good for a drama; more precisely, it is generally bad. The principle at issue is simple: art demands concentration; an artist cannot possibly be at his best if he attempts two things at one time. As a rule he is nearly at his worst; witness *Hard Times* (novel plus pamphlet); or (to come nearer to the present matter) witness the *Supplices* and the *Heracleidae*. Jebb thought he had hit on a word that cleared Sophocles at one stroke—'ideal'. Euripides in his definitely Athenian plays was being too obviously political; Sophocles, though we see his mind veering all the time to Athens, 'is an artist working in a purely ideal spirit'.[1] It is a question, I

[1] *Sophocles: The Oedipus Coloneus* (1907), p. xxxix.

think, of degree, and also of artistic skill. Sophocles had none of Euripides' recklessness and must have winced at some of his brother dramatist's procedures. His patriotic suffusion is delicate, he contrives his propaganda tactfully. But propaganda it essentially is, and 'the less Sophocles he' —as a dramatist—because he lets us see what he thinks about Athens. Nor is the harmony always so unassailable as Jebb would have us believe. In that exchange between Theseus and Creon the secondary intention is obvious: Theseus and Creon are like dummies, and the interview becomes faintly comic.

Any distraction in a drama is bad, and anything that does not minister to a drama is distraction. Still, readers too have their weaknesses, and we are not sorry that Sophocles relaxed: that he brought us, this once, so close to himself; that he let us hear, beneath the words of the play, the beating of his own heart.

WORKS CITED

AGARD, W. R. '*Antigone* 904-20', *Classical Philology* (Chicago), XXXII, No. 3, 1937, pp. 263-5.

BLUMENTHAL, A. W. von. *Sophokles*, 1936.

BOWRA, C. M. *Sophoclean Tragedy*, 1944.

BRADLEY, A. C. *Oxford Lectures on Poetry*, 1911.

—— *Shakespearean Tragedy*, 1904.

BULLINGER, A. *Der Endlich Entdeckte Schlüssel zum Verständniss der Aristotelischen Lehre von der Tragischen Katharsis*, 1878.

BYWATER, I. *Aristotle on the Art of Poetry*, 1909.

CAMPBELL, LILY. *Shakespeare's Tragic Heroes*, 1931.

CROISET, M. *Œdipe-Roi de Sophocle*, 1931.

FREEMAN, KATHLEEN. 'The Dramatic Technique of the *Oedipus Coloneus*', *Classical Review*, XXXVII, 1923, pp. 50-4.

FYFE, W. H. *Aristotle's Art of Poetry*, 1940.

GODDARD, H. 'In Ophelia's Closet', *Yale Review*, Spring 1946.

GREENE, W. C. *Moira*, 1944.

GRUBE, G. M. A. *The Drama of Euripides*, 1941.

GUDEMAN, A. *Aristoteles Poetik*, 1934.

HARRY, J. E. *Greek Tragedy*, 1933.

HARSH, P. W. *A Handbook of Classical Drama*, 1944.

JEBB, R. C. *The Tragedies of Sophocles, Translated into English Prose*, 1904.

—— *Sophocles: The Ajax*, 1896.
　　　　　　　The Antigone, 1906.
　　　　　　　The Oedipus Coloneus, 1907.
　　　　　　　The Philoctetes, 1890.
　　　　　　　The Trachiniae, 1892.

WORKS CITED

KAIBEL, G. *Elektra*, 1896.

KIRKWOOD, G. M. 'Two Structural Features of Sophocles' *Electra*', *Transactions and Proceedings of the American Philological Association*, LXXIII, 1942, pp. —.

KITTO, H. D. F. *Greek Tragedy*, 1939.

MAUGHAM, W. S. *The Summing Up*, 1938.

MILTON, J. *Samson Agonistes*, 1671.

MURRAY, G. *Greek Studies*, 1946.

NORWOOD, G. *Greek Tragedy*, 1920.

OWEN, A. S. 'The End of Sophocles' *Electra*', *Classical Review*, XLI, No. 2, 1927, pp. 50-2.

PAGE, D. L. *Actors' Interpolations in Greek Tragedy*, 1934.

PEVSNER, N. 'The Architecture of Mannerism', *The Mint*, ed. G. Grigson, 1946, pp. 116-38.

POHLENZ, M. *Die griechische Tragödie*, 1930.

RAWLINSON, G. *The History of Herodotus: A New English Version*, 1858-60.

REINHARDT, C. *Sophokles*, 1933.

ROBERT, C. *Oidipus*, 1915.

SHEPPARD, J. T. *The Oedipus Tyrannus of Sophocles*, 1920.

—— *The Wisdom of Sophocles*, 1947.

—— '*Electra:* A Defence of Sophocles', *Classical Review*, XLI, No. 1, 1927, pp. 2-9.

—— '*Electra* Again', *Classical Review*, XLI, No. 5, 1927, pp. 163-5.

THOMSON, G. *Aeschylus and Athens*, 1941.

VERRALL, A. W. *Four Plays of Euripides*, 1905.

WEBSTER, T. B. L. *An Introduction to Sophocles*, 1936.

WILAMOWITZ, T. von. *Die Dramatische Technik des Sophokles*, 1917.

WILSON, E. *The Wound and the Bow*, 1941.

WYCHERLEY, R. E. 'Sophocles *Antigone* 904-20', *Classical Philology* (Chicago), XLII, No. 1, 1947, p. 51.

INDEX

Titles of Sophocles' plays have been abbreviated as follows: *Ant.—Antigone; El.—Electra; OC.—Oedipus Coloneus; OT.—Oedipus Tyrannus; Ph.—Philoctetes; Tr.—Trachiniae.*

231